# ENGLISH THROUGH LITERATURE

## 文学で学ぶ英語リーディング

斎藤兆史・中村哲子［編注］
EDITED AND ANNOTATED BY SAITO YOSHIFUMI AND NAKAMURA TETSUKO

KENKYUSHA

# まえがき

　本書は、文学作品に現れる英文、あるいは文学的な要素を持つ英文を教材として英語を勉強するための教科書です。学習者のレベルとしては、平均的な大学1, 2年生を想定していますが、英語力次第では高校生にも十分使用が可能です。また、使用状況としては、大学の一般的な語学の授業を想定して作りました。セッションの数を15としたのも、大学の半期の授業を意識してのことです。もちろん、ほかの使い方も十分に可能ですし、英語独習用の教材として使っていただくこともできると思っています。

　日本の英語教育が昭和後期に実用コミュニケーション重視へと大きく舵を切って以来、英語の教材として文学的な文章を用いることはめっきり少なくなりました。文学に現れる英語は「コミュニケーション」の役に立たない古くさい言葉であると考えられ、逆に英語による自己紹介、買い物、道案内、あるいはオーラル・プレゼンテーションなどに用いられる表現が「実用的」な英語として注目されています。

　しかしながら、人と人のコミュニケーションは、ただの事務的なやり取りだけではなく、会話の中で使われる言葉も、かならずしも一義的に意味が確定するものばかりではありません。言語コミュニケーションが高度になるほど、私たちはさまざまな修辞法や文彩を操っています。そう考えると、日常言語と文学言語との境目もそれほど明確でないということがわかります。さらに、私たちが日常的に文学的な言語を操り、そもそも母語習得においてすらそのある部分でかならず文学に触れていることを考えれば、むしろ英語教材のどこかに文学的な内容のものがあるほうがむしろ自然なのです。

　1980年代から、とくにイギリスの文体論の学界を中心として、文学を積極的に英語教育に取り入れるための研究がさかんになってきました。英米では、文学教材の使い方もさまざまに工夫されています。残念ながら、日本においては、最近になって実用コミュニケーション偏重の教育に対する反省が始まり、それと同時に文学教材に対する再評価の機運が少しずつ高まっているとはいえ、文学教材を用いつつ多様な学習活動を可能ならしめる教科書の開発は、かならずしも目覚ましい進歩を遂げたとは言えない状況です。むしろ、文学教材の有効性は多くの教師が認識していながら、それを教室で用いるための方法論が明確に示されてこなかったのが実情です。私たちは、そのような状況を打開すべく、文学を用いた英語教育というアイデアを現場の授業に活かすための研究を進めてきました。この教科書は、そのような研究から生まれたものです。

　本書の使い方としては、基本的に毎回1セッションずつ、Pre-Reading, Reading Focus, Post-Readingを参考にしながらテキストを丹念に読み進めていただければいいかと思いま

す。Session 1 から順番どおりに読み進めていただいても結構ですし、1 つのジャンルに焦点を当てて教えるなど、目的に応じて臨機応変に使っていただければと思います。課業についても、音読、素読、暗唱、訳読、文法解析、ロール・プレイ、あるいは視聴覚教材との併用など、さまざまな工夫をしていただくべく、教材の使い方を限定するような指示は最小限に留めました。逆に言えば、あまり手を加えずとも、素材の良さで楽しめるテクストを選んだつもりです。15 セッションの素材では不十分である場合も考え、同じ趣旨で用いることのできるテクストを巻末にまとめて載せておきました。適宜ご利用いただければと思います。学習者の皆さんには、本書で英語を勉強することによって、文学を通じて英語を勉強することの、そして文学を読むことの楽しさを理解していただきたいと思っています。さらには、文化的なコミュニケーションも可能ならしめる、色合い豊かな英語を操る能力を養っていただくこともできると確信しています。

　本書の執筆と編集は、日本英文学会関東支部英語教育・学習研究会のなかで、とくに文学を英語教育に応用するための方法論を研究している後述のメンバーが、何度も会合を重ねながら慎重に行ないました。具体的な作業としては、Session 1 と 2 については北と斎藤が、Session 5, 8, 12 は深谷が、Session 9 は久世と中村が、Session 14 は坂野が主として担当し、残りの session については、他のメンバーが持ち寄った教案を活かす形で中村と斎藤が担当しました。また、企画・製作段階で研究社の星野龍氏と津田正氏にはたいへんお世話になりました。津田氏には、教案に関する貴重なご意見も多々いただきました。この紙面を借りて、お二人に謝意を表したいと思います。

　平成 21 年 9 月

編者代表　斎藤兆史

**執筆者・執筆協力者**（五十音順、肩書は令和元年 7 月現在）

奥　聡一郎　　関東学院大学教授
北　和丈　　　東京理科大学准教授
久世恭子　　　東洋大学准教授
斎藤兆史　　　東京大学名誉教授
関戸冬彦　　　白鷗大学教授
髙橋和子　　　明星大学教授
中村哲子　　　駒澤大学教授
坂野由紀子　　成蹊大学教授
深谷素子　　　鶴見大学教授

# 目次

まえがき ...................................................................................................................... iii

**Session 1** **Introduction**
文学の手ほどきとしての言葉遊び ............................................................... 1

**Session 2** **Language of Humor**
笑いのツボを理解する ................................................................................ 5

**Session 3** **George Bernard Shaw, *Pygmalion***
戯曲の英語で会話と発音を学ぶ ................................................................ 9

**Session 4** **Japanese Stories in Translation: Kenji and Ryunosuke**
日本語の作品を英訳で読む ...................................................................... 14

**Session 5** **Suzanne Vega, "Luka"**
歌詞に隠された物語を読む ...................................................................... 19

**Session 6** **Two Autobiographies: Martin Luther King and Ellen Glasgow**
自分の思い出を語る .................................................................................. 22

**Session 7** **Graham Greene, *A Sort of Life***
小説風の自伝を読む .................................................................................. 27

**Session 8** **Raymond Carver の短編小説**
小説の結末部分を読む .............................................................................. 33

**Session 9** **Haiku and Japanese Poems**
言葉のリズムを楽しもう .......................................................................... 37

**Session 10** **Four Types of Poetry**
気軽に英詩を楽しもう .............................................................................. 42

v

| | | |
|---|---|---|
| Session 11 | **Tennessee Williams, *A Streetcar Named Desire*** <br> 会話の意図をつかみ取る | 48 |
| Session 12 | **Benjamin Franklin, "Thirteen Virtues" and "Poor Richard's Maxims"** <br> モットーを書く | 54 |
| Session 13 | **Tim O'Brien, "Ambush"** <br> 事実と虚構の狭間を読む | 57 |
| Session 14 | **Lori Peikoff, "Table for Two"** <br> 逸話を語る | 62 |
| Session 15 | **Charles Dickens, *Great Expectations*** <br> 名作の原文を読む | 67 |
| **Appendix** | | 73 |

**コラム**　コックニーなまり　12 / 小説と映画・ドラマを使った「語り」の学習　32 / ナーサリー・ライムの世界　40 / 英詩の形式　47 / 文学的素養は究極のコミュニケーション・ツール　66

# Session 1

Introduction

## ―文学の手ほどきとしての言葉遊び―

### Pre-Reading

　文学の言語というと、私たちが日常的に使っているものとは違う何か特殊な言語であるような気がします。たしかに、単語1つを取っても、そこにいろいろな意味合いを込めることがあります。たとえば、本書の最後の教材となるチャールズ・ディケンズの『大いなる遺産』の原題は *Great Expectations* ですが、この expectations には「遺産」という意味と主人公の「期待」という意味が掛かっていると言われています。また、物語を読むときには、行間を読んだり、主題を考えたりしなければなりません。

　しかしながら、改めて考えてみると、私たちは日常的に洒落を言ったり、1つの言葉に複数の意味を込めてみたり、言葉遊びを交えながらコミュニケーションを図っています。高度なレベルの会話やスピーチになれば、修辞技巧を操ることもあります。そう考えると、私たちが日常的に使っている言語と文学の言語、もしくは文学的な言語との厳密な区別は難しいようです。

　この session では、文学的な言語使用の手ほどきとして、言葉遊びを含む文章を読んでみましょう。Text 1 は、ネイティブ・スピーカー同士の実際の会話に現れたやり取りとして Ronald Carter, *Investigating English Discourse: Language, Literacy and Literature*（Routledge, 1997）の中に紹介されているもの、Text 2 と 3 は広告に現れた英文、Text 4 はニュースの見出し、5つ目はリメリック（limerick）と呼ばれる滑稽詩です。

## ◉ Reading Focus ◉

1. ヒントを参考にして、それぞれの英文にどのような遊びが込められているのかを考えてみましょう。
2. 下線を引いた英語を辞書で調べ、文章のなかでどのような意味で使われているか、文字通りの意味と文脈に沿った意味を確認し、複数の意味が掛かっているかどうかを調べてみましょう。

# Reading

### <Text 1>

*A*: Thanks, I won't forget this time. Till tomorrow OK?

*B*: Brian, can you see those pigs over my left shoulder, moving slowly across the sky . . .

[*A and B burst into laughter.*]

　ヒント：友人の A に少額のお金を貸している B が、忘れっぽい A に対してやんわりと返済を促した直後の会話。会話の裏に (And) pigs may [might, could] fly という慣用表現がある。

### <Text 2>

A Tissot isn't out of place for a second.

　ヒント：スイスの時計会社 Tissot の広告のキャッチフレーズ。補助的な状況として、写真家が Tissot の時計をつけて忙しく飛び回る様子が描かれている。2 つの下線部に、それぞれ別々の意味が掛かっている。

---

[1] **Till tomorrow OK?:**「明日まで待ってもらってもいい？」
[3] ***burst into laughter:***「どっと笑い出した」。ここでの burst は過去形。

## 1. Introduction

**<Text 3>**

The price of our pint bottle in your local bar should have fallen. Think of it as a windfall.

　ヒント：Bulmers というアイルランドのリンゴ酒（cider）の値下げに関する広告。背景には枝の先についている 2 個の熟したリンゴと Bulmers のボトルが並んでいる。

**<Text 4>**

Tiger tames the Masters

　ヒント：1997 年にプロ・ゴルファーのタイガー・ウッズ（Tiger Woods）がゴルフのトーナメント大会の 1 つ、マスターズで優勝したときのニュースの見出し。tame という動詞が、通例だれが何に対して行なう行為を表わすものであるのかがわかれば、主語が Tiger で目的語が the Masters になっていることの面白さに気づくはず。

**<Text 5>**

A collegiate damsel named Breeze,

Weighed down by B.A.'s and Litt. D.'s,

　　Collapsed from the strain.

　　Alas, it was plain.

She was killing herself by degrees.

---

[1] **pint bottle:**「パイント瓶」。ここでは 1 パイント（約 0.57 *l*）入りのリンゴ酒の瓶を指している。
[1] **local bar:**「地元のバー」
[1] **should have fallen:**「下がったはずだ」。第一義的には、製造元が値下げをしたのだから、それぞれのバーで安くなっているはずだ、値引きがされていないとしたらそれは間違いだ、という意味だが、商品がリンゴ酒であり、広告に熟れたリンゴの写真が載っていることで、また別のイメージを喚起する。
[1] **Think of ... as 〜:**「...を〜と考えてください」。ここでは命令文だが、think of A as B は「A を B と見なす」の意。
[2] **the Masters:** = the Masters Tournament. アメリカで行なわれる世界的に有名なゴルフの大会。ただし、ここでの Masters には別の意味が掛かっている。
[3] **collegiate damsel:**「女子大生」。大仰な表現だが、滑稽詩という文脈と韻律を考えての選択だと思われる。
[3] **Breeze:** これも女性の名前としては変わっているが、韻と関係がある。
[4] **B.A.:** Bachelor of Arts の略、「学士号」。
[4] **Litt. D.:** Litterarum Doctor の略、「文学博士号」。
[5] **Collapsed from the strain:**「重圧に耐えられずに倒れた」
[6] **Alas, it was plain:**「ああ、（残念ながら）理由は明らかだ」

ヒント：2行目のB.A.とLitt.D.を表わすdegreesの意味と、by degreesという慣用句の意味に注意。

## Post-Reading

1. Text 1 において、Bが、明日借りた金を返すと言っているAの約束を信用しているかどうかを考えましょう。
2. Text 2 の out of place, for a second それぞれの違った意味を掛け合わせると、文全体が2つの違った意味を持つ文になります。それを説明しなさい。
3. Text 3 の windfall をリンゴと考えた場合と値引きと考えた場合で、2文目が2つの違った意味を持ちます。その言葉遊びを説明しなさい。
4. Text 4 の Tiger には、タイガー・ウッズと虎の2つの意味が掛かっていますが、the Masters には、ゴルフ・トーナメントのほかにどのような意味が掛かっていると思いますか。
5. Text 5 の各行末に注目すると、音に関して一定の規則があることがわかります。どのような規則があるかを説明しなさい。
6. Text 5 の面白さを説明しましょう。

# Session 2

Language of Humor

## ―笑いのツボを理解する―

### Pre-Reading

　私たちは毎日のように言葉のやり取りのなかで笑ったり笑わせたりしています。ユーモアは、日常的な言語コミュニケーションの重要な一部なのです。

　とはいえ、ユーモアを理解したり操ったりするには、意外なことに、かなり高度な語学力が必要です。英語による日常的なやり取りは理解できるのに、英語の冗談を理解したり、英語で冗談を言ったりするのが難しいと感じている日本人は少なくないでしょう。というのも、ユーモアの文体を理解するためには、その言語構造はもちろんのこと、文化的背景や言外の意味など、さまざまなことを一瞬のうちに読み取る必要があるからであり、また冗談や笑い話で人を笑わせるためには、言葉にひねりや洒落を利かせるだけの言語技術がなければならないからです。気の利いた話で人を笑わせられるようになったら語学学習も卒業だと言われる所以です。

　この session では、ユーモアを表現する文章を読むことにします。Text 1〜5 は Fred Metcalf (ed.), *The Penguin Dictionary of Jokes* (1993) に収められた笑い話、Text 6 と 7 は地口 (pun) となぞなぞ (riddle)、Text 8 は、19世紀後半から20世紀初頭にかけてアメリカで活躍した作家アンブロウズ・ビアス (Ambrose Bierce, 1842–?1914) の手になる数々の風刺や皮肉を辞書の体裁にまとめた『悪魔の辞典』(*The Devil's Dictionary*, 1911) から取った定義文です。とりあえず、一通り読んで、それぞれを面白いと感じるかどうか確認してみましょう。

## ⊕ Reading Focus ⊕

それぞれの文章を読み、すぐに吹き出すほど面白いと感じたものには○、面白いとは思わなかったが笑いのツボが分かったものには△、何が面白いのかまったくわからなかったものには×をつけてみましょう。また、面白いと感じたものについては、どこが面白かったのかを考えてみましょう。

# Reading

**<Text 1>**

**SON**: Remember that vase you were always worried I might break?

**MOTHER**: What about it?

**SON**: Well, your worries are over.

**<Text 2>**

**A**: How did you break your arm?

**B**: Well, do you see that broken step? [5]

**A**: Yes.

**B**: Well, I didn't.

**<Text 3>**

**READER**: Can you tell me where the 'Self-help' section is?

**LIBRARIAN**: But doesn't that defeat the whole purpose?

**<Text 4>**

A company was looking to employ a new accountant and had called in the last three [10]

---

[1] **Remember . . . ?:** Do you remember . . . ? の短縮形。

[8] **'Self-help' section:** 日本語で言うところの「自己啓発本」など、自助や自立の仕方を教えてくれる本を英語で 'self-help book' と言う。ここでの 'Self-help' section は、図書館の中でそのような本が置いてあるコーナーを指している。

[10] **accountant:**「会計係」

candidates for their final interviews. The first candidate was invited into the chairman's office and asked, 'What's two plus two?'

'Four,' he replied.

The second candidate was invited in and she was asked, 'What's two plus two?'

She replied, 'Four.' [5]

Finally, the third candidate was invited in and he was asked, 'What's two plus two?'

He said, 'What do you want it to be?'

They said, 'You've got the job.'

### <Text 5>

On his first night in prison, a convict is glumly eating his dinner when another convict leaps to his feet, shouts 'Thirty-seven', and all the other inmates laugh hysterically. [10]

Later, another shouts, 'Four hundred and twenty', with exactly the same result.

'What's going on?' says the convict to his cell-mate, sitting next to him.

'It's like this: we only have one joke book in the prison and everyone knows all the jokes off by heart. So instead of telling the whole joke, we just stand up and shout a number.' [15]

A few days later, the new convict decides that it's time to try it out for himself. So he stands up and shouts, 'Fourteen.'

Silence.

Turning to his cell-mate, he asks, 'What went wrong?'

'Must be your delivery.' [20]

### <Text 6>

**Q.** What part of England has the most dogs?

**A.** Barkshire.

---

[12] **cell-mate:**「同房者」。同じ cell (監房) に入っている仲間ということ。
[14] **off by heart:**「すっかり暗記して」
[20] **Must be . . . :** It must be . . . の短縮形。
[20] **delivery:**「言い方、話し方」
[22] **Barkshire:** イングランドに実際に存在する Berkshire という土地の名前には、[bɔ́ːkʃə, (-ʃɪə)] と [báːkʃə, (-ʃɪə)] という違う発音が存在する。後者で発音すると、この洒落が成立する。

### <Text 7>

Three monks were passing

Three pears were hanging

Each took one

And that left two.

Question: How is this possible? [5]

Answer: One of the monks was named 'Each'.

### <Text 8>

**Circus,** *n*. A place where horses, ponies and elephants are permitted to see men, women and children acting the fool.

**Friendship,** *n*. A ship big enough to carry two in fair weather, but only one in foul.

**Hatred,** *n*. A sentiment appropriate to the occasion of another's superiority. [10]

**Misfortune,** *n*. The kind of fortune that never misses.

**Plan,** *v.t*. To bother about the best method of accomplishing an accidental result.

---

[9] **foul**: foul weather（悪天候）の weather が省略された形。直前の fair weather と対になっている。

### Post-Reading

1. それぞれの笑い話について、何が面白いのかを説明しなさい。
2. Text 1〜8と小説、戯曲、詩などの文学形式との共通点を考えてみましょう。
3. Text 8のスタイルを用いて、ユーモアの利いた定義文を書いてみましょう。

# Session 3
## George Bernard Shaw, *Pygmalion*
## ―戯曲の英語で会話と発音を学ぶ―

### Pre-Reading

　オードリー・ヘップバーン（Audrey Hepburn）主演のミュージカル映画『マイ・フェア・レディ』（*My Fair Lady*, 1964）を観たことのある人は少なくないでしょう。この映画の原作となったのが、ジョージ・バーナード・ショー（George Bernard Shaw, 1856–1950）というアイルランド生まれの劇作家の書いた『ピグマリオン』（*Pygmalion*, 初演 1913, 出版 1916）という戯曲です。なまりの強い英語を話すロンドンの花売り娘イライザ・ドゥーリトル（Eliza Doolittle [dúːlɪtl]）が音声学者ヘンリー・ヒギンズ（Henry Higgins）の発音指導を受けて上品な婦人に変身していくというプロットを中心として、恋愛、結婚、社会階級など、人間関係をめぐるさまざまな問題点を浮き彫りにしている作品です。この session では、この戯曲中、ヒギンズ先生による発音指導を描いた一節に注目します。

### ◎ Reading Focus ◎

1. イライザの発音の癖がどのようなものかを想像してみましょう。
2. 本文は、大きく分けて、場面を客観的に説明した物語文（narrative）、登場人物が発した台詞（speeches）、その台詞を発するときの登場人物の様子を示したト書き（stage directions）の3つの部分に分かれます。英文のどの部分がそれぞれに相当するのかを考えてみましょう。
3. それぞれの登場人物がどのような感情を込めながら台詞を発しているかを想像しながら読んでみましょう。

# Reading

There seems to be some curiosity as to what Higgins's lessons to Eliza were like. Well, here is a sample: the first one.

Picture Eliza, in her new clothes, and feeling her inside put out of step by a lunch, dinner, and breakfast of a kind to which it is unaccustomed, seated with Higgins and the Colonel in the study, feeling like a hospital out-patient at a first encounter with the doctors.

Higgins, constitutionally unable to sit still, discomposes her still more by striding restlessly about. But for the reassuring presence and quietude of her friend the Colonel she would run for her life, even back to Drury Lane.

**HIGGINS**: Say your alphabet.

**LIZA**: I know my alphabet. Do you think I know nothing? I dont need to be taught like a child.

**HIGGINS** [*thundering*]: Say your alphabet.

**PICKERING**: Say it, Miss Doolittle. You will understand presently. Do what he tells you; and let him teach you in his own way.

**LIZA**: Oh well, if you put it like that — Ahyee, bə yee, cə yee, də yee —

---

[3–4] **feeling her inside put out of step ... it is unaccustomed:**「慣れていないような昼食、夕食、朝食を食べて、お腹の調子が変になって」。it は inside を言い換えたもの。

[4–5] **the Colonel:** Higgins の友人である Pickering 大佐のこと。

[8] **But for ...:**「〜がなかったならば」。主節 (she would 以下) が仮定法過去の形をしているので、節で言い換えると、If it were not for ..., あるいは Were it not for ... となる。

[9] **run for her life:**「必死の思いで走って逃げる」。for one's life は、「命からがら、必死に」の意。

[9] **Drury Lane:** ロンドン中央部の通りで、もともとイライザが住んでいた貧困層居住地区にあたる。その名は、エリザベス朝期にこの地に大邸宅を構えていたドルリー家に由来する。この通り近くのドルリー・レーン劇場で演じられた初演に、劇場ミュージカル版の『マイ・フェア・レディ』がある。

[11] **LIZA:** Eliza の愛称。

[11] **dont** = don't. 本作のテクストでは、助動詞 + not の短縮形を示すアポストロフィが省略される。以下の cant, wont の表記においても同じ。

[13] **thundering:**「どなるように」。鍵括弧のなかにイタリックで書かれている部分がト書き。

[16] **Ahyee, bə yee, cə yee, də yee:** イライザの発音の癖を示すための特殊な表記。ə は schwa と呼ばれる発音記号。

## 3. George Bernard Shaw, *Pygmalion*

**HIGGINS** [*with the roar of a wounded lion*]: Stop. Listen to this, Pickering: This is what we pay for as elementary education. This unfortunate animal has been locked up for nine years in school at our expense to teach her to speak and read the language of Shakespeare and Milton. And the result is Ahyee, Bə-yee, Cə-yee, Də-yee. [*To Eliza*] Say A, B, C, D. [5]

**LIZA** [*almost in tears*]: But I'm saying it. Ahyee, Bə-yee, Cə-yee —

**HIGGINS**: Stop. Say a cup of tea.

**LIZA**: A cappətə-ee.

**HIGGINS**: Put your tongue forward until it squeezes against the top of your lower teeth. Now say cup. [10]

**LIZA**: C-c-c — I cant. C-Cup.

**PICKERING**: Good. Splendid, Miss Doolittle.

**HIGGINS**: By Jupiter, she's done it at the first shot. Pickering: we shall make a duchess of her. [*To Eliza*] Now do you think you could possibly say tea? Not tə-yee, mind: if you ever say bə-yee cə-yee də-yee again you shall be dragged round the room three [15] times by the hair of your head. [*Fortissimo*] T, T, T, T.

**LIZA** [*weeping*]: I cant hear no difference cep that it sounds more genteel-like when you say it.

**HIGGINS**: Well, if you can hear that difference, what the devil are you crying for? Pickering: give her a chocolate. [20]

**PICKERING**: No, no. Never mind crying a little, Miss Doolittle: you are doing very well; and the lessons wont hurt. I promise you I wont let him drag you round the room by your hair.

---

[3] **at our expense:**「我々の金を使って」。at ～'s expense は、「～の出費で」の意。
[3-4] **the language of Shakespeare and Milton:** もちろん英語のことだが、シェイクスピアとミルトンの名前を出しているのは、せっかくの格調高い言語がイライザの発音によって台無しになっていることを強調するため。
[13] **By Jupiter:** ＝by Jove「おやまあ」。ここでは驚きを表している。
[13] **at the first shot:**「1 回（の試み）で」
[13-14] **make a duchess of her:**「彼女（イライザ）を公爵夫人（のような貴婦人）にする」
[17] **cep** ＝ except.

**HIGGINS**: Be off with you to Mrs Pearce and tell her about it.  Think about it.  Try to do it by yourself: and keep your tongue well forward in your mouth instead of trying to roll it up and swallow it.  Another lesson at half-past four this afternoon.  Away with you.

*Eliza, still sobbing, rushes from the room.* [5]

And that is the sort of ordeal poor Eliza has to go through for months before we meet her again on her first appearance in London society of the professional class.

---

[1] **Be off with you:**「行きなさい」
[1] **Mrs Pearce:** 独身者 Higgins の身の回りの世話をするメイド。
[7] **London society of the professional class:**「ロンドンの知識人階級の社交界」

## Post-Reading

1. 第2段落冒頭の 'Picture Eliza'（10頁3行目）は、だれの、だれに対する言葉かを考えてみましょう。
2. Higgins の6番目の台詞中に現れる 'you shall be dragged round the room three times by the hair of your head'（11頁、15–16行目）を和訳してみましょう。
3. 発音記号を参照しながら、正しい発音でアルファベットを丁寧に発音してみましょう。
4. それぞれの登場人物の気持ちを考えながら、台詞を読み分けてみましょう。

## 3. George Bernard Shaw, *Pygmalion*

● **Column 1** ●

### コックニーなまり

　Pre-Reading で触れたミュージカル映画『マイ・フェア・レディ』のなかで、オードリー・ヘップバーン扮するイライザが、'The rain in Spain stays mainly in the plain'、それから 'In Hartford, Hereford and Hampshire hurricanes hardly ever happen' という文句を絡めて歌を歌う場面があります。それぞれ「スペインの雨は主に平原に降る」、「ハートフォードとヘリフォードとハンプシャーでは、ハリケーンはめったに起こらない」という意味ですが、彼女はなぜそのような歌詞の歌を歌っているのでしょうか。

　じつは、この2文は、イライザの発音を矯正するためのものなのです。もともとロンドンのなかでも労働者階級の人が多く住むイースト・エンド地区あたりで話されていた英語のなまりを「コックニーなまり」(Cockney accent) と言いますが、その特徴として、標準英語の [eɪ] が [aɪ] のように発音され (さらに標準英語の [aɪ] は [ɔɪ] のようになります)、語頭の [h] の音が落ちる傾向があります。典型的なコックニーなまりの話者であるイライザは、標準英語の [eɪ] が正しく発音できるようになるまで、また語頭の [h] がきちんと出るようになるまで、[eɪ] と [h] の音を多く配したこの2文をひたすら唱えつづけるのです。ちなみにこの2つの文は、1938年に制作された映画の『ピグマリオン』の中ではすでに用いられていますが、原作には現れません。

# Session 4

Japanese Stories in Translation: Kenji and Ryunosuke

# ―日本語の作品を英訳で読む―

## Pre-Reading

　日本語で書かれた小説を積極的に英訳で読む日本人はそれほど多くないかもしれません。ですが、きわめて多くの日本語の作品が次々と英訳される時代となり、海外の本屋で日本人作家の本がずらりと店頭に並んでいるのを見て、これほど多くの人に読まれているのかと実感することがあります。

　いったい日本語の語り口やニュアンスが英語でうまく伝えられるのかと疑問に思う人もいるでしょう。実際にどのように英訳されているのかは、興味が湧くところです。そこで、宮沢賢治と芥川龍之介のよく知られた物語を読み、英語でどのような語りがなされているか味わってみましょう。まず、「注文の多い料理店」(1924) では、宮沢賢治らしい擬音語・擬態語を盛り込んだ語り口がどのように英語に移されているか楽しみましょう。次に、芥川龍之介の「蜘蛛の糸」(1918) を読み、原作の独特な語り口がどのように翻訳に反映されているかに眼を向けます。翻訳とは、原作で書かれている内容をそのまま別の言語で書き換えることではないことがわかってくるでしょう。英語で書かれたもう1つの物語世界をのぞいてみましょう。

## Reading Focus

1. 物語を語る日本語の口調を活かすためにどのような工夫がなされているかを考えてみましょう。
2. 英語で書かれた作品として、その文学的な表現を味わいましょう。

# 4. Japanese Stories in Translation: Kenji and Ryunosuke

# **Reading**

**&lt;Text 1&gt;** "The Restaurant of Many Orders," translated by John Bester (1993)

"Yes, hurry up! The boss has his napkin tucked in and his knife in his hand and he's licking his lips, just waiting for you."

But the two young gentlemen just wept and wept and wept and wept.

Then, all of a sudden, they heard a *woof, woof,* and a *grr*! behind them, and the two dogs like white bears came bursting into the room. The eyes behind the keyholes disap- [5] peared in a twinkling. Round and round the room the dogs rushed, snarling, then with another great *woof*! they threw themselves at the other door. The door banged open, and they vanished inside as though swallowed up. From the pitch darkness beyond came a great miaowing and spitting and growling, then a rustling sound.

The room vanished in a puff of smoke, and the two young gentlemen found themselves [10] standing in the grass, shivering and shaking in the cold. Their coats and boots, purses and tiepins were all there with them, hanging from the branches or lying among the roots of the trees. A gust of wind set the grass stirring, the leaves rustling, and the trees creaking and groaning.

原　作
「早くいらつしやい。親方がもうナフキンをかけて、ナイフをもつて、舌なめずりして、お客さま方を待つてゐられます。」
　二人は泣いて泣いて泣いて泣いて泣きました。
　そのときうしろからいきなり、

---

[1] **Yes, hurry up!:** 山奥に狩りにやってきた主人公2人だが、食事をしようと Restaurant Wildcat House に入ったところ、料理を食べるのが自分たちではなく、ここの主人の wildcat であることに気づく。手下の1人が下ごしらえのできた2人をせかせ、主人の前に連れて行こうとするところ。

[1] **tucked in:** tuck in ～で、「～の端をどこかに挟んで固定する」。

[3] **the two young gentlemen:** この箇所は原作では「二人」だが、物語の冒頭で「二人の若い紳士」として登場する。

[5] **The eyes behind the keyholes:** 1つの扉に大きな鍵穴が2つあり、これまで wildcat の青い眼玉がきょろきょろと部屋をのぞいているのが見えていた。

[8] **as though swallowed up:** = as though they had been swallowed up.

[8] **pitch darkness:**「まっくらやみ」

「わん、わん、ぐわあ。」といふ声がして、あの白熊のやうな犬が二疋、扉をつきやぶつて室の中に飛び込んできました。鍵穴の眼玉はたちまちなくなり、犬どもはううとうなつてしばらく室の中をくるくる廻つてゐましたが、また一声
「わん。」と高く吠えて、いきなり次の扉に飛びつきました。戸はがたりとひらき、犬どもは吸ひ込まれるやうに飛んで行きました。
　その扉の向ふのまつくらやみのなかで、
「にやあお。くわあ、ごろごろ。」といふ声がして、それからがさがさ鳴りました。
　室はけむりのやうに消え、二人は寒さにぶるぶるふるへて、草の中に立つてゐました。
　見ると、上着や靴や財布やネクタイピンは、あつちの枝にぶらさがつたり、こつちの根もとにちらばつたりしてゐます。風がどうと吹いてきて、草はざわざわ、木の葉はかさかさ、木はごとんごとんと鳴りました。

### <Text 2>　"The Spider Thread," translated by Jay Rubin (2006)

A.　第1節冒頭――御釈迦様の登場

And now, children, let me tell you a story about Lord Buddha Shakyamuni.

It begins one day as He was strolling alone in Paradise by the banks of the Lotus Pond. The blossoms on the pond were like perfect white pearls, and from their golden centers wafted forth a never-ending fragrance wonderful beyond description. I think it must have been morning in Paradise. [5]

原　作

　ある日の事でございます。御釈迦様は極楽の蓮池のふちを、独りでぶらぶら御歩きになっていらっしゃいました。池の中に咲いている蓮の花は、みんな玉のようにまっ白で、そのまん中にある金色の蕊からは、何とも云えない好い匂が、絶間なくあたりへ溢れて居ります。極楽は丁度朝なのでございましょう。

B.　第2節冒頭――犍陀多の物語のはじまり

Here, with the other sinners at the low-point of the lowest Hell, Kandata was endlessly floating up and sinking down again in the Pond of Blood. Wherever he looked

---

[2] **He:** 御釈迦様であるため、神様を示すときの習慣にしたがってHを大文字にしている。
[4] **wonderful beyond description:** fragranceを修飾する形容詞句。

there was only pitch darkness, and when a faint shape did pierce the shadows, it was the glint of a needle on the horrible Mountain of Needles, which only heightened his sense of doom. All was silent as the grave, and when a faint sound did break the stillness, it was the feeble sigh of a sinner. As you can imagine, those who had fallen this far had been so worn down by their tortures in the seven other hells that they no longer had the [5] strength to cry out. Great robber though he was, Kandata could only thrash about like a dying frog as he choked on the blood of the pond.

And then, children, what do you think happened next? Yes, indeed: raising his head, Kandata chanced to look up toward the sky above the Pond of Blood and saw the gleaming silver spider thread, so slender and delicate, slipping stealthily down through the [10] silent darkness from the high, high heavens, coming straight for *him*! Kandata clapped his hands in joy. If only he could take hold of this thread and climb up and up, he could probably escape from Hell. And maybe, with luck, he could even enter Paradise. Then he would never again be driven up the Mountain of Needles or plunged down into the Pond of Blood. [15]

No sooner had the thought crossed his mind than Kandata grasped the spider thread and started climbing with all his might, higher and higher. As a great robber, Kandata had had plenty of practice at this kind of hand-over-hand rope climbing.

## 原　作

　こちらは地獄の底の血の池で、ほかの罪人と一しょに、浮いたり沈んだりしていた犍陀多でございます。何しろどちらを見ても、まっ暗で、たまにそのくら暗からぼんやり浮き上っているものがあると思いますと、それは恐しい針の山の針が光るのでございますから、その心細さと云ったらございません。その上あたりは墓の中のようにしんと静まり返って、たまに聞えるものと云っては、ただ罪人がつく微かな嘆息ばかりでございます。これはここへ落ちて来るほどの人間は、もうさまざまな地獄の責苦に疲れはてて、泣声を出す力さえなくなっているのでございましょう。ですからさすが大泥坊の犍陀多も、やはり血の池の

---

[1] **a faint shape did pierce the shadows:** shadows は複数形で「暗闇」のこと。ここでは、ときとして針の山の金属がわずかな光に反射し、その姿が闇を貫くような姿で現れる様子を示す。

[5] **the seven other hells:** 仏教では八大地獄という概念がある。

[17] **with all his might:**「全力で」

[18] **hand-over-hand:** ロープを持つ手の上のほうにもう一方の手を伸ばしてつかみ、たぐり寄せる様子を示す。

血に咽びながら、まるで死にかかった蛙のように、ただもがいてばかり居りました。

　ところがある時の事でございます。何気なく犍陀多が頭を挙げて、血の池の空を眺めますと、そのひっそりとした暗の中を、遠い遠い天上から、銀色の蜘蛛の糸が、まるで人目にかかるのを恐れるように、一すじ細く光りながら、するすると自分の上へ垂れて参るのではございませんか。犍陀多はこれを見ると、思わず手を拍って喜びました。この糸に縋りついて、どこまでものぼって行けば、きっと地獄からぬけ出せるのに相違ございません。いや、うまく行くと、極楽へはいる事さえも出来ましょう。そうすれば、もう針の山へ追い上げられる事もなくなれば、血の池に沈められる事もある筈はございません。

　こう思いましたから犍陀多は、早速その蜘蛛の糸を両手でしっかりとつかみながら、一生懸命に上へ上へとたぐりのぼり始めました。元より大泥坊の事でございますから、こう云う事には昔から、慣れ切っているのでございます。

## Post-Reading

1. Text 1の原作では、動物の鳴き声や風の音などを表現するために擬音語・擬態語が多く使われています。すべての擬音語・擬態語に下線を引き、それぞれどのように訳されているか確認しなさい。
2. Text 1の英訳から1つのパラグラフを自由に選び、原作を見ないで日本語に訳しなさい。グループごとにすべてを訳し、他のグループの訳と比較してみてもいいでしょう。
3. Text 2のA.とB.の英訳を読み、物語の提示の仕方が原作とはどのように違うか確認しなさい。また、その理由についても考えてみましょう。
4. Text 2のB.の末尾から3行目にある "the thought"（17頁16行目）の内容が示されている箇所を確認しなさい。
5. Text 2のB.で、英訳するのに表現を工夫したと思われる箇所を挙げ、どのように工夫されているか話し合ってみましょう。

# Session 5
Suzanne Vega, "Luka"

## ―歌詞に隠された物語を読む―

### Pre-Reading

　英語の歌というと、どうしてもリズムやメロディに注目してしまい、歌詞カードを丹念に読むなどということはしないものです。愛の告白のつもりでサビのメロディを口ずさんでいたら、実は反戦ソングだったなどということもあります。そこで、この session では、歌詞の英語をじっくり読み、そこに隠された物語を発見してみましょう。

　スザンヌ・ヴェガ (Suzanne Vega, 1959– ) の「ルカ」("Luka") は、1987年に発表され日本でも大ヒットしました。アコースティックなサウンドに乗って、つぶやくような歌声が聞こえてきます。歌詞の内容を理解したら、今度は一緒に歌ってみましょう。話すのと変わらないような調子で歌えるので、英語の話し言葉のリズムをつかむのにとてもいい練習になります。

### Reading Focus

1. 歌詞であるために、語り手ルカについての情報が具体的にわかるように書かれてはいません。単に英語を理解するだけではなく、ルカの気持ちに寄り添って、英文から少しでも多くのことを感じ取ってみましょう。
2. スザンヌ・ヴェガの歌をよく聞き、弱く速く発音している箇所に注意しながら、歌のリズムに合わせて歌ってみましょう。

# Reading

## "Luka"     Suzanne Vega

My name is Luka
I live on the second floor
I live upstairs from you
Yes I think you've seen me before

If you hear something late at night                                      [5]
Some kind of trouble, some kind of fight
Just don't ask me what it was
Just don't ask me what it was
Just don't ask me what it was

I think it's because I'm clumsy                                          [10]
I try not to talk too loud
Maybe it's because I'm crazy
I try not to act too proud

They only hit until you cry
And after that you don't ask why                                         [15]
You just don't argue anymore

---

[3] **upstairs from you:** 前置詞が from であることに注意。
[10] **clumsy:** moving or doing things in a careless way, especially so that you drop things, knock into things etc (*Longman Dictionary of Contemporary English*).
[13] **proud:** feeling pleased about something that you have done or something that you own, or about someone or something you are involved with or related to (*Longman Dictionary of Contemporary English*).
[16] **argue:** to disagree with someone in words, often in an angry way (*Longman Dictionary of Contemporary English*).

## 5. Suzanne Vega, "Luka"

You just don't argue anymore
You just don't argue anymore

Yes I think I'm okay
I walked into the door again
Well, if you ask that's what I'll say [5]
And it's not your business anyway
I guess I'd like to be alone
With nothing broken, nothing thrown

Just don't ask me how I am
Just don't ask me how I am [10]
Just don't ask me how I am

---

[4] **walked into the door:** よそ見をしていて、そこにドアがあると気づかずにドアにぶつかること。
[6] **business:** something that concerns a particular person or organization (*Oxford Advanced Learner's Dictionary of Current English*).
[8] **With nothing broken, nothing thrown:** 付帯状況の with の構文。

### Post-Reading

1. 次の歌詞の意味を説明しなさい。
    a. I think it's because I'm clumsy（20 頁 10 行目）
    b. I try not to act too proud（同 13 行目）
    c. You just don't argue anymore（同 16 行目）
2. Luka についてわかることや想像できること（年齢、性別、性格、今の心理状態、生活環境など）を列挙してみましょう。
3. この歌のテーマを説明しなさい。
4. 第 5 スタンザの "Yes I think I'm okay ... it's not your business anyway"（21 頁 3–6 行目）を、Luka の気持ちを表すように日本語に翻訳しなさい。さらに、そのときの Luka の気持ちを説明してみましょう。
5. この歌に込められた思いが伝わるように、歌ってみましょう。

# Session 6

Two Autobiographies: Martin Luther King and Ellen Glasgow

## ―自分の思い出を語る―

### Pre-Reading

　文学作品の1つのジャンルに自伝や伝記があります。自伝は日記と同様に1人称で語られるもので、ルソーの『告白』（執筆 1765–70; 出版 1782, 1788）以降、自分のことを語る伝統は小説の隆盛ともあいまって、英語圏でも19世紀半ばには確立されます。現在では、各分野で成功を収めた人だけでなく、多くの人が自分の人生を総括するために自分史を書くようになってきました。だれでも、幼い頃のある経験が現在の自分に影響を与えていると感じることがあるでしょう。

　この session では、自分の小さな頃の思い出を語った文章を味わい、現在の自分が過去のできごとを語る表現方法を学びます。最終的には、短いエピソードを英語で書いてみたいものです。Text 1 は、"I have a dream" のスピーチで有名なキング牧師（Martin Luther King, Jr., 1929–68）の自伝、『マーティン・ルーサー・キング自伝』（*The Autobiography of Martin Luther King, Jr.*, 1998）の第1章からの抜粋。Text 2 は、ヴァージニア州で一生を過ごしたピューリッツァー賞受賞作家、エレン・グラスゴー（Ellen Glasgow, 1873–1945）の『内なる女性』（*The Woman Within*, 1954）と題された自伝、第4章からの抜粋です。それぞれの書き方の特徴を的確につかみたいものです。

### Reading Focus

1. 思い出を書くときの型を知り、その人らしさが感じられるような書き方がどのようなものか読んで味わいましょう。
2. 文章を読むときには、読み取ったことを応用して文章が書けるように、書くつもりで読みましょう。

## 6. Two Autobiographies: Martin Luther King and Ellen Glasgow

# Reading

### <Text 1>

Two incidents happened in my late childhood and early adolescence that had a tremendous effect on my development. The first was the death of my grandmother. She was very dear to each of us, but especially to me. I sometimes think I was her favorite grandchild. I was particularly hurt by her death mainly because of the extreme love I had for her. She assisted greatly in raising all of us. It was after this incident that for the first time [5] I talked at any length on the doctrine of immortality. My parents attempted to explain it to me, and I was assured that somehow my grandmother still lived. I guess this is why today I am such a strong believer in personal immortality.

The second incident happened when I was about six years of age. From the age of three I had a white playmate who was about my age. We always felt free to play our [10] childhood games together. He did not live in our community, but he was usually around every day; his father owned a store across the street from our home. At the age of six we both entered school — separate schools, of course. I remember how our friendship began to break as soon as we entered school; this was not my desire but his. The climax came when he told me one day that his father had demanded that he would play with me [15] no more. I never will forget what a great shock this was to me. I immediately asked my parents about the motive behind such a statement.

We were at the dinner table when the situation was discussed, and here for the first time I was made aware of the existence of a race problem. I had never been conscious of it before. As my parents discussed some of the tragedies that had resulted from this prob- [20] lem and some of the insults they themselves had confronted on account of it, I was greatly shocked, and from that moment on I was determined to hate every white person.

---

[1–2] **that had a tremendous effect on my development:** two incidents を修飾する関係代名詞節。
[6] **at any length:**「少しでも」
[11] **our community:** 黒人コミュニティのこと。
[13] **separate schools:** 白人と黒人で通学する学校が異なっていた。
[17] **motive:** 行動の根拠となるその人自身の考え。motivation とは語義が異なる。
[21] **on account of it:** on account of = because of、it = this problem。
[22] **from that moment on:**「そのとき以降ずっと」

As I grew older and older this feeling continued to grow.

My parents would always tell me that I should not hate the white man, but that it was my duty as a Christian to love him. The question arose in my mind: How could I love a race of people who hated me and who had been responsible for breaking me up with one of my best childhood friends? This was a great question in my mind for a number of years. [5]

### <Text 2>

In my seventh summer I became a writer. As far back as I remember, long before I could write, I had played at making stories, and, in collaboration with Mammy, I had created Little Willie and his many adventures. But not until I was seven or more, did I begin to pray every night "O God, let me write books! Please, God, let me write books!" [10]

One summer day, lying on the blue grass at Jerdone Castle, beneath sweeping boughs of the "old elm," which was so large that it took five of us to measure its bole, I found myself singing aloud in time with the wind in the leaves. Beyond the clustering leaves, I could see the sky as blue as the larkspur in the field below the garden fence, and over the blue a fleet of small white clouds was sailing. [15]

"I would that I with the clouds could drift," I began to sing under my breath. "Qui-

---

[2] **My parents would always tell me that . . . :** would は過去の習慣を表す。
[4] **breaking me up with 〜:** 〜から私を引き裂くこと。
[8] **Mammy:** ＝黒人の乳母。Lizzie Jones という人物。
[9] **Little Willie and his many adventures:** 創作した物語のこと。Little Willie は主人公の名前。
[9–10] **did I begin:** 副詞節の not until I was seven or more が前に置かれているため、I began ではなく did I begin となる。
[11] **Jerdone Castle:** 1742 年にプランテーションとして開かれた土地の名称で、1879 年にエレン・グラスゴーの父親が別荘としてこの地所を購入した。本宅はリッチモンドにあり、一家は毎年夏をこの別荘で過ごした。
[12] **"old elm":** 引用符によって、この木を通常こう呼んでいたことを示している。
[12] **it took five of us to measure its bole:** 幹の太さは 5 人が手を広げて囲むほどであったということ。
[13] **in time with the wind in the leaves:**「木の葉を渡る風に合わせて」
[15] **a fleet of small white clouds was sailing:** a fleet of 〜（乗り物）＝〜の一団。clouds を船に見たてて was sailing を使っている。fleet には「艦隊」の意味もあり、was sailing の縁語となっている。
[16] **I would that I with the clouds could drift:** ＝I wish that I could drift with the clouds. 詩では、韻律などを優先し、ときとして句の位置を入れ替えたりすることがある。
[16] **under my breath:**「小声で」

## 6. Two Autobiographies: Martin Luther King and Ellen Glasgow

etly, happily onward — " And then suddenly, with a start of surprise, I exclaimed aloud, "But that's po'try! That's po'try! And I made it!" Joy flooded through me. Running into the house, I seized a paper and pencil from my sister's desk, and came back to the elm, while the rhythm ran on and on and on in my thoughts, making a new hymn — a hymn of my very own. [5]

    Drift from this land of mist and snow,

    Drift to the land where I long to go,

    Leaving behind me the world's sad choices,

    Hearing alone the angels' voices,

    At the foot of my Father's throne. [10]

"That's po'try," my heart sang over and over, "and I wrote it!"

  For days my new happiness lasted, as if I had entered some hidden forest of wonder and delight. I wandered "lonely as a cloud" in that strange exile to which all writers who are born and not made are condemned. Then the end came with a shock that plunged me from joy into despair. One morning, seeking more paper and a sharpened pencil in my [15] sister's room, I heard her voice reading my precious verses aloud to her guests, and I overheard, too, the burst of kindly ridicule and amusement. Noiselessly, without the flutter of a curtain, I fled back through the window, and down the columns of the porch to the shelter of the big box-bush beneath. My skin felt naked and scorched, as if a flame had blown over it. [20]

  Was that the beginning of my secrecy, I have sometimes wondered. Was the sensitiveness I have always felt about my work rooted in the sharp mortification of that awakening?

---

[1] **with a start of surprise:**「はっと驚いて」

[2] **po'try:** = poetry.

[10] **my Father's throne:**「父なる神の御座」

[13] **I wandered "lonely as a cloud":** ウィリアム・ワーズワースの有名な詩の第1行、I wandered lonely as a cloud（詩のタイトルも同名）を念頭に置いている。

[13] **strange:**「未知の」

[14] **condemned: condemn ～(人) to ...** =「...という不愉快な状況に、運命的に～を導く」

[18] **the columns of the porch:**「張り出し玄関の柱」

[19] **box-bush:** = boxwood（西洋ツゲ）。生垣などに用いられる潅木。

[21] **Was that the beginning of my secrecy, I have sometimes wondered.:** = I have sometimes wondered if that was the beginning of my secrecy.

## Post-Reading

1. Text 1を構成する4つのパラグラフの内容について、それぞれ簡潔な日本語に要約しなさい。そのうえで、パラグラフ間の関係がどのようになっているか確認しましょう。文章の流れやパラグラフの関係性を明確に示す表現に下線を引いておくとよいでしょう。
2. Text 1で動詞が過去形以外の時制となっているのはどのような場合か、説明しなさい。
3. Text 2の第1～3パラグラフに見られるすべての節について、主語に下線を引き、どのような主語が使われているかを把握しなさい。そのさい、1文の主語になっているものには○も付け、1文全体のどこに位置しているかを確認しましょう。文の構造を明確に認識できるはずです。
4. Text 1と2の思い出の書き方について、類似点と相違点を箇条書きに列挙してみましょう。
5. 自分の幼いときの思い出を1つ、本文を参考にしながら英語で書きましょう。

# Session 7

Graham Greene, *A Sort of Life*

## ―小説風の自伝を読む―

### Pre-Reading

　実用的なコミュニケーションというと、買い物や道案内など、簡単な口頭でのやり取りですぐに結果や答えが与えられる類の会話を思い浮かべがちですが、私たちが日常的に行なっている言語コミュニケーションのかなりの部分は、昨日どこで何をしたとか、いつだれがどこで何をしたとか、自分が見聞した出来事を伝える物語（narrative）が占めています。その中でも一番語る頻度が高いのは、当然ながら自分に関する物語です。すでに前の session で自伝の文章をいくつか読みましたが、この session では、会話の部分が小説風に脚色された自伝の文章を読んでみましょう。

　本文は、『落ちた偶像』（*The Fallen Idol*, 1948）、『第三の男』（*The Third Man*, 1949）という名作映画の脚本や、『ブライトン・ロック』（*Brighton Rock*, 1938）、『権力と栄光』（*The Power and the Glory*, 1940）、『事件の核心』（*The Heart of the Matter*, 1948）、『情事の終り』（*The End of the Affair*, 1951）などの「カトリック小説」で知られるグレアム・グリーン（Graham Greene, 1904–91）の自伝『ある種の人生』（*A Sort of Life*, 1971）から取りました。グリーンの作品には、物語自体の娯楽性に関わりなく「追跡」のモチーフが頻繁に現れますが、ここで取り上げる一節にも「追う者」対「追われる者」という図式が皮肉な形で見られます。

### Reading Focus

1. 友人の身の上話を聞くような気持ちで、話のオチを想像しながら読んでみましょう。
2. 自分が主人公だったらどのような感情を抱くかを考えてみましょう。

# Reading

 While I was at St John's I must have read Q's novel *Foe-Farrell* three or four times. It was the dramatic story of a man's revenge, and I very much wanted an opportunity for dramatic revenge. As I remember the tale a political demagogue ruined the experiment of a great surgeon by inciting a mob to wreck his laboratory where it was believed that he was practicing vivisection. From that moment the surgeon Foe (or was it Farrell?) pursued [5] Farrell (or was it Foe?) across the world and through the years with the sole object of revenge — I think he even found himself alone in an open boat on the Pacific with his enemy, improbable though this may sound. Then, under the long-drawn torture of the pursuit, the characters changed places: the pursued took on nobility, the pursuer the former vulgarity of his enemy. It was a very moral story, but I don't think it was the [10] moral which interested me — simple revenge was all I wanted.

 For there was a boy at my school called Carter who perfected during my fourteenth and fifteenth years a system of mental torture based on my difficult situation. Carter had an adult imagination — he could conceive the conflict of loyalties, loyalties to my age-

---

[1] **St John's:** = St John's house. イングランドのハートフォードシャー州にあるカトリック系のバーカムステッド・スクールの建物の1つ。

[1] **Q's:** Q はイギリスの作家 Sir Arthur Quiller-Couch (1863–1944) の筆名。

[3] **As I remember the tale:**「その物語について私が覚えているところによれば」。これに続く主節の部分で、語り手たるグリーンが記憶に基づいて物語のあらすじを説明している。

[3] **political demagogue:**「煽動政治家」

[5] **vivisection:**「生体解剖」

[5] **Foe (or was it Farrell?) ... :** 題名にもなっている主要登場人物2人の名前のうち、どちらの人物がどちらの名前だったか、グリーンの記憶が今ひとつ定かでない。実際には、外科医の名前が Foe で間違いない。また、Foe という名前には、普通名詞の foe（敵、仇）の意味が掛かっていることにも注意。

[9] **the pursued took on nobility:**「追われているほうが高潔になって」。「定冠詞 the ＋過去分詞」（あるいは形容詞）で、「〜の人」という意味になることがある。

[12] **For:** 前に述べたことの理由や根拠を挙げるときに用いる等位接続詞。ここでは、グリーンが *Foe-Farrell* に特別な興味を持った裏に少年時代の体験があることを示す役割を果たしている。従属接続詞の because とは用法が違うことに注意。

[13] **my difficult situation:** グリーンの父親はこの学校の校長であり、兄はその学事長をしている。イギリス国教会を国教とする国において、父親と兄がカトリック系の学校の首脳部にいるという複雑な事情がこの話の背景にある。

## 7. Graham Greene, *A Sort of Life*

group, loyalty to my father and brother. The sneering nicknames were inserted like splinters under the nails.

I think in time I might have coped with Carter — there was an element of reluctant admiration, I believe, on both sides. I admired his ruthlessness, and in an odd way he admired what he wounded in me. Between the torturer and the tortured arises a kind of [5] relationship. So long as the torture continues the torturer has failed, and he recognizes an equality in his victim. I never seriously in later years desired revenge on Carter. But Watson was another matter.

Watson was one of my few friends, and he deserted me for Carter. He had none of Carter's *finesse* — Carter continually tempted me with offers of friendship snatched [10] away like a sweet, but leaving the impression that somewhere some time the torture would end, while Watson imitated him only at a blundering unimaginative level. Alone he would have had no power to hurt. Nonetheless it was on Watson that I swore revenge, for with his defection my isolation had become almost complete.

For many years after leaving school, when I thought back to that period, I found the [15] desire for revenge alive like a creature under a stone. The only change was that I looked under the stone less and less often. I began to write, and the past lost some of its power — I wrote it out of me. But still every few years a scent, a stretch of wall, a book on a shelf, a name in a newspaper, would remind me to lift the stone and watch the creature move its head towards the light. [20]

---

[1–2] **like splinters under the nails:**「爪の中に刺さったとげのように」。Carter があだ名に込める辛辣な悪意を表わす比喩。
[10] ***finesse:***「巧妙さ」
[10–11] **tempted me with offers of friendship snatched away like a sweet:**「友達として仲良くしてくれそうな甘い顔をしたかと思うと、お菓子をさっと引っ込めるようにそのいつわりの友情を取り去ってしまうのだった」
[12–13] **Alone he would have had no power to hurt:**「独力では人に苦痛を与えることなどできなかったであろう」。過去の反実仮想を表す仮定法過去完了。副詞の alone が、「もし～であったなら」の意味を表す if 節と同じ機能を果たしている。
[18] **wrote it out of me:**「書くことでそれ（＝過去）を自分のなかから抜いてしまった」
[18–19] **a scent, a stretch of wall, a book on a shelf, a name in a newspaper, would remind me to...:**「ちょっとした匂い、壁、本棚においた本、新聞で見た名前によって記憶が呼び起こされ、～する気になったものだ」。何かのきっかけで昔の復讐心がまたふつふつと湧いてくるありさまを描いている。ここでの would は、過去の（不規則な）習慣を表す助動詞。

In December 1951 I was in the shop of the Cold Storage Company in Kuala Lumpur buying whisky for Christmas which I was going to spend in Malacca. I had just got back from a three-day jungle patrol with the 2/7th Gurkha Rifles in Pahang, seeking communist guerillas, and I was feeling very tired of Malaya. A voice said, 'You are Greene, aren't you?' [5]

A foxy-faced man with a small moustache stood at my elbow.

I said, 'Yes, I'm afraid . . .'

'My name's Watson.'

'Watson?' It must have been a very long time since I had lifted the stone, for the name meant nothing to me at first, nor the flushed colonial face. [10]

'We were at school together, don't you remember? We used to go around with a chap called Carter. The three of us. Why, you used to help me and Carter with our Latin prep.'

At one time, in the days when I still day-dreamed, I would imagine meeting Watson at a cocktail party and in some way humiliating him in public. Nothing could have been [15] more public than the Cold Storage Company of Kuala Lumpur during the Christmas rush, but all I could find to say was, 'I didn't think I was any good at Latin.'

'Better than we were anyway.'

I said, 'What are you doing now?'

'Customs and excise. Do you play polo?' [20]

'No.'

'Come along and see me play one evening.'

'I'm just off to Malacca.'

'When you get back. Talk over old times. What inseparables we were — you and me

---

[1] **Cold Storage Company:** 冷蔵や冷凍を必要とする食品を商う店。
[2] **Malacca:** マレー半島南西部の港町ムラカ（Melaka）のこと。1824年よりイギリスの領有が始まり、第2次世界大戦後までその影響力が残った。
[3] **the 2/7th Gurkha Rifles:**「第二、第七グルカ・ライフル銃隊」
[3] **Pahang:**「パハン州」。現マレーシアの内陸部に位置する。
[4] **Malaya:** マレー半島南端にあったイギリスの旧植民地。現在のマレーシアの一部。
[13] **prep:** 〈英〉「宿題」
[20] **Customs and excise:** = the Board of Customs and Excise.「関税消費税局（の仕事）」。

and old Carter.' It was obvious that his memory held a quite different impression from mine.

'What's happened to Carter?'

'He went into Cables and died.'

I said, 'When I get back from Malacca . . .' and went thoughtfully out. [5]

What an anti-climax the meeting had been. I wondered all the way back to my hotel if I would ever have written a book had it not been for Watson and the dead Carter, if those years of humiliation had not given me an excessive desire to prove that I was good at something, however long the effort might prove. Was that a reason to be grateful to Watson or the reverse? I remembered another ambition — to be a consul in the Levant: [10] I had got so far as sitting successfully for the *viva*. If it had not been for Watson . . . So speculating, I felt Watson sliding out of mind, and when I came back from Malacca I had forgotten him.

Indeed it was only many months later, after I had left Malaya, as I thought, for good, that I remembered I had never rung him up, had never watched him play polo, nor ex- [15] changed memories of the three inseparables. Perhaps, unconsciously, that was my revenge — to have forgotten him so easily. Now that I had raised the stone again, I knew that nothing lived beneath it.

---

[4] **Cables:**「電信部隊」
[7] **had it not been for Watson and the dead Carter:** = if it had not been for . . . .「もしもワトソンと死んだカーターがいなかったら」。仮定法過去完了の主節を導く従属節。
[10] **the Levant:**「レバント地方（地中海東岸地域）」
[11] ***viva:*** = viva voce.「口頭試問、面接試験」

## Post-Reading

1. 第2段落の 'he could conceive the conflict of loyalties, loyalties to my age-group, loyalty to my father and brother'（28頁14行〜29頁1行目）の意味を説明しなさい。
2. 語り手は Carter と Watson にどのようにいじめられたのか、また、同様にいじめられたにしても、なぜ Watson に対してのみ復讐心を抱いたのか、Carter と Watson の違いに注目して考えましょう。

3. 語り手がどのような復讐の場面を思い描いていたかを説明しなさい。
4. 最後から2段落目の冒頭の一文 'What an anti-climax the meeting had been.'（31頁6行目）を和訳しなさい。
5. この逸話を通じて現れる stone と creature の比喩が何を表わしているのかを説明しなさい。

● Column 2 ●

### 小説と映画・ドラマを使った「語り」の学習

　本書には、実話とフィクションの中間にあるようなテクストがいくつか収められています。このような文章をたくさん読み、何度も音読することで、英語で自分のことを語ることが上手になります。

　本書では取り上げなかった作品のなかで、とくに上記の目的に適うものとして、日系イギリス人作家カズオ・イシグロ（Kazuo Ishiguro, 1954– ）の小説があります。代表作がすべて主人公の「私」語りで書かれており、『遠い山なみの光』（*A Pale View of Hills*, 1982）、『浮世の画家』（*An Artist of the Floating World*, 1986）など、日本が舞台になっていたり、日本人が登場したりする小説があるので、情景を思い浮かべながら勉強をすることができます。

　イシグロ作品のなかでも、とくにお勧めしたいのが、ブッカー賞受賞作品『日の名残り』（*The Remains of the Day*, 1989）です。イギリス人執事が自分の半生を回想するという体裁の小説で、物語がとてもよくできています。舞台はイギリスですが、格調高い口語表現がたくさん出てきますので、上品な英語を覚えたい人の学習には最適です。ただし、やや丁寧すぎる「執事言葉」もたくさん出てくるので、あまりこの小説の文体が板についてしまうと、イギリス人に「あなたは執事みたいなしゃべり方をしますね」と言われてしまうかもしれません。もっとも、そこまでの英語が話せるようになれば上等です。

　『日の名残り』は、ジェイムズ・アイヴォリー（James Ivory）監督によって映画化されました。名優アンソニー・ホプキンズ（Anthony Hopkins）とエマ・トンプソン（Emma Thompson）が中心人物を演じている名画であり、これも勉強のさいの参考になるでしょう。ただし、映画化にさいしての必然的な処理として、原作では読者に対して虚々実々の語りを仕掛ける姿の見えない主人公が、映画では一人の登場人物としてこちらからはっきり見える位置に置かれています。そのような原作との違いは違いとして楽しむとして、台詞回しなどは大いに参考になると思います。

# Session 8
Raymond Carver の短編小説

# ―小説の結末部分を読む―

## Pre-Reading

　小説をどのように締めくくったらよいか、作家たちはさまざまな工夫を凝らして、読者の心に残るようなエンディングを生み出します。ハッピーエンディングかオープンエンディングか、その終わり方で小説そのものの質も変わってきます。短編小説の結末部分を読み、エンディングの重要性について考えてみましょう。

　レイモンド・カーヴァー（Raymond Carver, 1938–88）は、1980 年代アメリカで活躍した短編作家です。日本では、村上春樹の翻訳によって広く知られるようになりました。貧しい家庭に生まれ、19 歳で結婚し、子育てをしながら創作活動を続けます。短編作家を志したのも、日々の生活に追われながらなんとか捻出した短い時間で、1 つの作品を集中して書き上げられるからでした。

　アルコール中毒や肺ガンに苦しめられたカーヴァー。レーガン政権が掲げる「強いアメリカ」の陰でひっそりと、しかし粘り強く生きるアメリカの貧しい労働者階級に、彼は温かい目を注ぎ続けました。

## Reading Focus

1. この結末部分では、登場人物の内面に関する描写がほとんど見られません。彼ら 3 人の行動や短い言葉の端々から、三者三様の心持ちを考えながら読みましょう。
2. この結末部分にいたるまでにどのような展開があったのか、想像しながら読みましょう。

# Reading

It was warm inside the bakery. Howard stood up from the table and took off his coat. He helped Ann from her coat. The baker looked at them for a minute and then nodded and got up from the table. He went to the oven and turned off some switches. He found cups and poured coffee from an electric coffee-maker. He put a carton of cream on the table, and a bowl of sugar. [5]

"You probably need to eat something," the baker said. "I hope you'll eat some of my hot rolls. You have to eat and keep going. Eating is a small, good thing in a time like this," he said.

He served them warm cinnamon rolls just out of the oven, the icing still runny. He put butter on the table and knives to spread the butter. Then the baker sat down at the table [10] with them. He waited. He waited until they each took a roll from the platter and began to eat. "It's good to eat something," he said, watching them. "There's more. Eat up. Eat all you want. There's all the rolls in the world in here."

They ate rolls and drank coffee. Ann was suddenly hungry, and the rolls were warm and sweet. She ate three of them, which pleased the baker. Then he began to talk. They [15] listened carefully. Although they were tired and in anguish, they listened to what the baker had to say. They nodded when the baker began to speak of loneliness, and of the sense of doubt and limitation that had come to him in his middle years. He told them what it was like to be childless all these years. To repeat the days with the ovens end-

---

[2] **He helped Ann from her coat.:**「彼はアンがコートを脱ぐのに手を貸した」
[9] **the icing still runny:** 焼きたてで熱いため、砂糖がけがとろりと溶けたままである。
[13] **There's all the rolls in the world in here.:** all と in the world によって、食べたいパンは何でも出してあげるという気持ちを表している。
[19] **To repeat the days with the ovens endlessly full and endlessly empty.:** 主語と述語動詞がないので、節ではなく句。with は付帯状況を示す。なお、意味的には、前文の to be childless all these years と並置されているが、ここで間接話法から自由間接話法に移行し、このパラグラフの終わりまでパン屋の話し言葉の語調が生かされた英文が続く。

lessly full and endlessly empty. The party food, the celebrations he'd worked over. Icing knuckle-deep. The tiny wedding couples stuck into cakes. Hundreds of them, no, thousands by now. Birthdays. Just imagine all those candles burning. He had a necessary trade. He was a baker. He was glad he wasn't a florist. It was better to be feeding people. This was a better smell anytime than flowers. [5]

"Smell this," the baker said, breaking open a dark loaf. "It's a heavy bread, but rich." They smelled it, then he had them taste it. It had the taste of molasses and coarse grains. They listened to him. They ate what they could. They swallowed the dark bread. It was like daylight under the fluorescent trays of light. They talked on into the early morning, the high, pale cast of light in the windows, and they did not think of leaving. [10]

---

[1–2] **Icing knuckle-deep.:** 砂糖がけがたっぷりとかかっていて、手を差し込むと指の付け根まで隠れるほどである。
[2] **tiny wedding couples:** ウェディングケーキに飾りとしてついている小さな作り物の花嫁花婿のこと。
[3–4] **a necessary trade:** 人々にとって必要な商売。
[6] **breaking open a dark loaf:** 食べやすいようにパンを割っている。a dark loaf は小麦以外の麦が使われた茶色のパン。
[9] **the fluorescent trays of light:** オフィスや教室でよく見かける、天井に付いている四角い形の蛍光灯の照明。
[10] **the high, pale cast of light in the windows:** 朝日が窓越しに高いところからうっすらと射してくる様子。light の後に being を補うとわかりやすい。

## Post-Reading

1. パン屋が Ann と Howard に話を始める場面（They ate rolls and drank coffee. . . . that had come to him in his middle years. 34 頁 14–18 行目）では、この夫婦の様子が描写されています。ここから、2 人の置かれている状況や心持ちを推理しなさい。
2. パン屋が自分について語る場面で（To repeat the days. . . . This was a better smell anytime than flowers. 34 頁 19 行目—35 頁 5 行目）は自由間接話法と呼ばれる話法によって、話し手の語調がわかるように書かれています。この部分をパン屋の台詞のように、日本語に翻訳しなさい。
3. パン屋の台詞にある "Eating is a small, good thing in a time like this"（34 頁 7–8 行目）について、a time like this とはどのような時であるか推測してみ

ましょう。
4. この結末部分にいたるまでの物語のストーリーを自分なりに想像し、その展開を説明しなさい。その根拠が本文のどこにあるかも指摘しましょう。
5. 本文中に使われている語句を用いて、この短編小説にふさわしいタイトルをつけなさい。その後で、この小説全体を読んで確認するのもいいでしょう。
6. 小説の最後で、Ann と Howard について "they did not think of leaving." と書かれています。このときの2人の心情がどのようなものであったかを考えてみましょう。

# Session 9

Haiku and Japanese Poems

## ―言葉のリズムを楽しもう―

### Pre-Reading

　詩には欠かせない要素の1つとして、声に出して読んだときに感じられる音の響きのおもしろさや美しさがあります。多くの日本人が、『百人一首』の短歌1つ1つの意味を深く考える前に口で覚え、そのリズムの心地よさを体感した経験を持っていることでしょう。

　短歌よりも限られた文字数で拡がりのある世界を語る詩、俳句。実は haiku として世界に知られ、多くの人たちがさまざまな言語で haiku をひねっています。それも、芭蕉の俳句を筆頭に多くの句がすぐれた英訳で紹介され、高い評価を得たことによります。むろん、現代詩も数多く英訳されており、英訳詩集の書評が海外の一流誌に登場したりすることもあります。

　ここでは、まず、芭蕉の『奥の細道』(1694)から1句取り上げ、3つの英訳を比べます。次に、谷川俊太郎の詩、「『飢餓』のためのメモランダ」(1980)から言葉遊びの様相を呈している一節を取り上げます。最後に、中原中也の「サーカス」(1934)の一節を読み、聞きなれない日本語表現がどのように英訳されているかに目を向けます。意味よりも、音の響きが醸し出すニュアンスが命とも言える俳句や詩が、どのような英語表現に移し替えられているでしょうか。

### Reading Focus

1. 日本の俳句や詩の雰囲気を伝えるために、英訳ではどのような工夫がなされているかを考えましょう。
2. 繰り返し音読して、英語の詩としてのリズムや雰囲気を味わいましょう。

# Reading

### <Text 1>

翻訳 A.

the stillness —

soaking into stones

cicada's cry

　　　　　— Translated by William J. Higginson & Penny Harter (1985)


翻訳 B.

How still it is here —

Stinging into the stones,

The locusts' trill

　　　　　— Translated by Donald Keene (1955)


翻訳 C.

What stillness! The cicadas' voices

Penetrate the rocks.

　　　　　— Translated by Asataro Miyamori (1932)


翻訳 D.

Up here, a stillness —

the sound of the cicadas

seeps into the crags.

　　　　　— Translated by Arthur Binard (2005)


原　作　　閑さや岩にしみ入蝉の声

9. Haiku and Japanese Poems

<Text 2>

Famishing,
they farmed.

Farming,
they famished.

In famishing there is farming; [5]
in farming, famishing.
— From 'Notes for "Starvation",' translated by William I. Elliott and Kazuo Kawamura (1986)

原　作

飢えて
植えた

植えて
飢えた

飢えには植えがある
植えには飢えがある

<Text 3>

High overhead, from the big top's crossbeam,
　　hangs one flying trapeze, [10]
　　　　just a wisp of a trapeze.

---

[4] **famish:** 自動詞で「飢える」。
[6] **in farming, famishing:** = in farming there is famishing.
[9] **crossbeam:** サーカスのテントの天井近くに渡された大梁。
[10] **trapeze:**「空中ブランコ」
[11] **a wisp of ～:** 長く細いものの様子を示す。

Then the trapeze artist swings out, upside down,
　arms dangling under the stained canvas ceiling,
　　SEEEEEEE SAAAAAAW, SEE and SAW.
　　　— From 'Circus,' translated by Arthur Binard (2007)

原　作

サーカス小屋は高い梁(はり)
　そこに一つのブランコだ
見えるともないブランコだ

頭倒(さか)さに手を垂れて
　汚れ木綿の屋蓋(やね)のもと
ゆあーん　ゆよーん　ゆやゆよん

---

[1] **the trapeze artist:**「空中ブランコ曲芸師」。the はこの小さなサーカス団の花形曲芸師であることを示す。

## Post-Reading

1. Text 1 の英訳を読んで、俳句の五、七、五の形式がどのように移し替えられているか確認しなさい。次に、単語、文法構造、音の響きやリズムの違いに目を向け、4つの英訳のニュアンスがどのように違うかを考えてみましょう。英和辞書や英英辞書を活用するとよいでしょう。
2. Text 2 の英訳と原作を比較しながら読み、まず、英語と日本語の根本にある構造的な違いが何であるか考えましょう。次に、訳者が単語、詩形、文型の選択において原作のエッセンスを伝えようと工夫した点は何かを考えてみましょう。
3. Text 3 の英訳を読み、英語としてどのような構造になっているか説明しなさい。
4. Text 3 の最終行、'SEEEEEEE SAAAAAAW, SEE and SAW' とはどのようなイメージを与える表現か考えてみましょう。

## 9. Haiku and Japanese Poems

● Column 3 ●

### ナーサリー・ライムの世界

　言葉のリズムを楽しむ詩として英語圏で最も親しまれているものに、日本ではマザー・グース（Mother Goose）として知られているナーサリー・ライム（Nursery Rhymes）があります。日本の「ずいずいずっころばし」や「かごめかごめ」といったわらべ歌のように、長年歌い継がれてきた伝承童謡ですが、その多くは18世紀に広まったものです。節に合わせてからだを動かしながら歌うもので、子供が言葉のリズムを体感し、言語感覚を養う一助となっています。その内容は、数え歌、遊び歌、子守唄、早口やなぞなぞなどと多岐にわたり、意味の不明確な表現や、意味の通らない「ナンセンス」も盛り込まれています。よく知られた2つの詩を紹介しましょう。

| | |
|---|---|
| See-saw, Margery Daw, | シーソー、マージョリー・ドー、 |
| Jacky shall have a new master; | ジャッキーにゃ新しい親方がいい、 |
| Jacky shall have but a penny a day, | ジャッキーにゃ1日1ペニーでいい、 |
| Because he can't work any faster. | だってちっともさっさとできないからさ。 |

　子どもたちがシーソー遊びをするときによく歌われる歌。なお、Margery Daw は女性の名前。

| | |
|---|---|
| Humpty Dumpty sat on a wall, | ハンプティー・ダンプティーが塀のうえ |
| Humpty Dumpty had a great fall. | ハンプティー・ダンプティーが転げ落ちた |
| All the king's horses, | 王さまの馬がみんなかかっても |
| And all the king's men, | 王さまの家来がみんなかかっても |
| Couldn't put Humpty together again. | ハンプティーをもとどおりにゃもどせなかった |

　なぞかけの詩で、ルイス・キャロル（Lewis Carroll, 1832–98）の『鏡の国のアリス』（*Through the Looking-Glass*, 1871）にも登場し、そのさし絵とともに広く知られている。

# Session 10

Four Types of Poetry

## ―気軽に英詩を楽しもう―

### Pre-Reading

　英詩というとどうも構えてしまう人が多いのではないでしょうか。英語がピンとこないとか、細かい規則を知らなければよく理解できないといった思いを抱きやすいことは確かです。しかしながら、英語圏では、日々の生活の中に英詩が身近なものとして入り込んでいて、パーティのような集まりで英詩の朗読がなされたり、poetry reading の会がしばしば開かれたりします。あるいは、Session 1 で紹介したような limerick を座興で作って宴席を盛り上げるようなこともあります。また、スコットランドやアイルランドで、詩人と呼ばれる人たちがその芸術活動を積極的に社会にアピールしている様子には驚かされることも少なくありません。

　ただし、一口に詩と言っても、さまざまなものがあります。上述の limerick をはじめ、ユーモアを含んだ短い詩もあれば、人間存在の根幹に関わる深い洞察を含んだものもあります。また、叙情的な内容のものもあれば、物語を語る叙事詩もあります。形式的に見ても、韻律をきちんと守る詩もあれば、自由な形式の詩もあります。さらには、文字配列の視覚的・図像的な面白さで読ませる concrete poetry と呼ばれるものもあります。

　ここでは、4種類の違った詩を読むことで、英詩の世界の豊かさに触れてもらおうと思います。Text 1 はアイルランドで人気の高いブレンダン・ケネリー（Brendan Kennelly, 1936– ）の最新詩集『声の群像』（*Reservoir Voices*, 2009）からの小品3点、Text 2 はロバート・ピンスキー（Robert Pinsky, 1940– ）というアメリカ詩人の 'ABC' (2000) と題する light verse, Text 3 はシーグフリード・サスーン（Siegfried Sassoon, 1886–1967）の戦争詩 'They' (1917), Text 4 はイギリスの桂冠詩人ウィリアム・ワーズワース（William Wordsworth, 1770–1850）の作品の中でもとりわけ有名な 'My Heart Leaps Up'（執筆 1802, 出版 1807）という詩です。

## 10. Four Types of Poetry

### Reading Focus
1. 詩においては行末が文の切れ目ではないことに注意し、それぞれの詩の意味を考えましょう。
2. 言葉の響きを楽しみながら繰り返し音読し、詩の世界を満喫しましょう。

# Reading

<Text 1>　　From *Reservoir Voices*, by Brendan Kennelly

**A. 'Football'**

Girls and boys, young men and women
chase me with a vigour
not many know or knew

but nobody on earth
enjoys being kicked around　　　　　　　　　　　　　　　　　[5]
like I do.


**B. 'Secret'**

If I were to tell you
the essence of what I am
I would be
the kind of traitor　　　　　　　　　　　　　　　　　　　　　[10]
most repulsive
to my own nature.

---

[題名] **Football:** イギリス英語で football が何を指すかを確認のこと。
[3] **not many know or knew:** 行頭に関係代名詞の that を補うとわかりやすい。
[11–12] **most repulsive / to my own nature:** traitor をうしろから修飾している。

## C. 'Sigh'

Whenever she heaves me now
I am no longer a mere sigh,
I am a story as well,

a story, however, that she,
for reasons far deeper than me, [5]
will never tell.

### <Text 2>

'ABC'　by Robert Pinsky

Any body can die, evidently. Few
Go happily, irradiating joy,

Knowledge, love. Many
Need oblivion, painkillers, [10]
Quickest respite.

Sweet time unafflicted,
Various world:

X = your zenith.

---

[4] **a story, however, that she,:** この行からの3行分は、前行の a story と同格の関係になっている。
[7] **Any body:** あえて2語に分けてあるところがミソ。
[8–9] **irradiating joy, / Knowledge, love:**「喜び、知恵、愛を振りまきながら」
[12] **unafflicted:** 直前の Sweet time に形容詞的にかかる過去分詞。afflicted の反意語。

## 10. Four Types of Poetry

### &lt;Text 3&gt;

'They'　by Siegfried Sassoon

The Bishop tells us: 'When the boys come back
They will not be the same; for they'll have fought
In a just cause: they lead the last attack
On Anti-Christ; their comrades' blood has bought
New right to breed an honourable race,　　　　　　　　　　　　　　　　[5]
They have challenged Death and dared him face to face.'

'We're none of us the same!' the boys reply.
'For George lost both his legs; and Bill's stone blind;
Poor Jim's shot through the lungs and like to die;
And Bert's gone syphilitic: you'll not find　　　　　　　　　　　　　　[10]
A chap who's served that hasn't found *some* change.'
And the Bishop said: 'The ways of God are strange!'

### &lt;Text 4&gt;

'My Heart Leaps Up'　by William Wordsworth

My heart leaps up when I behold
　　A rainbow in the sky:

---

[1] **Bishop:**「(英国国教会の) 主教」
[3] **just cause:**「正当なる大義名分」
[4] **Anti-Christ:**「反キリスト」。キリスト教国側から見れば、戦う敵はキリストの教えに背く存在として規定される。
[6] **him:** = Death.
[8] **Bill's stone blind:**「ビルは失明してしまっている」。Bill's = Bill is.
[9] **like to die:**「死にかけている」。ここでの like は「〜しそうで」の意の形容詞。
[10] **syphilitic:**「梅毒の」
[11] **A chap who's served:**「従軍した者は」。who's = who has.
[11] ***some:*** みんな「何かしらの変化 (= 被害、傷)」を被ったことが強調されている。

So was it when my life began;

So is it now I am a man;

So be it when I shall grow old,

   Or let me die!

The Child is father of the Man; [5]

And I could wish my days to be

Bound each to each by natural piety.

---

[1–3] **So was it when . . . / So is it now . . . / So be it when . . . :**「〜のときもそうであり、いまや〜となってもそうであり、〜のときもそうであれかし」

[5] **The Child is father of the Man:**「子供は大人の父である」。この詩の中でもとくに有名な命題。ロマン派における子供信仰を如実に表している。

[7] **natural piety:**「自然の恵みに対する敬虔な感謝の気持ち」

## Post-Reading

1. Text 1 の 3 作品で、まず、語り手 I が具体的に何であるのか確認しなさい。
2. Text 1 の 3 作品はすべて 1 文で成り立っています。各行が、構造的に文のどの部分に当たるのか確認しなさい。そのうえで、詩という表現形態が作品のおもしろさをどのように効果的に引き出しているかを考えましょう。
3. Text 2 がなぜ 'ABC' と題されているのかを考えましょう。
4. Text 3 がどのような韻律の規則にしたがっているかを説明しなさい。
5. Text 3 の主教の最後の言葉 'The ways of God are strange!' がどのような意味かを考えましょう。
6. Text 4 の詩の中で虹がどのような意味を持っているかを考えましょう。

## 10. Four Types of Poetry

● Column 4 ●

### 英詩の形式

　俳句や短歌が一定の規則に則って作られるように、英詩にも伝統的に受け継がれてきた詩形があります。日本語では、仮名1字が1つの母音を持つ1音節を形作っているため、俳句なら仮名17字で成り立ちます。ですが、英語では、1つの単語の音節数が異なるため、詩形は単語数でなく、音節数で整えます。

　よく見られる詩形として、1行の音節数が8や10に揃えられているものがあります。その音節の成り立ちを分析すると、弱く発音される音節と強く発音される音節のペアが4組、あるいは5組と連なっていて、詩人が単語のアクセントの位置をよく計算して1行を書いていることがわかります。この session の Text 3 は、音節のペアが5組となっている詩ですが、第1スタンザ（第1連のこと）の最終行の音節数のみ多くなっています。このように、パターンとのずれが見られることもあるのです。また、この詩では、各行末で同じ発音が規則的に繰り返され、スタンザごとに ababcc と韻を踏んでいることがわかります。

　実は、各行の音節数が異なり、1スタンザ全体で1つの型を形成している場合もあります。その1例として挙げられる詩形が、Session 1 の Text 5 に挙げたリメリックで、次のような型が基本となっています。

　　　（×）× / × × / × × /　　（脚韻 a）
　　　（×）× / × × / × × /　　（脚韻 a）
　　　　　（×）× / × × /　　（脚韻 b）
　　　　　（×）× / × × /　　（脚韻 b）
　　　（×）× / × × / × × /　　（脚韻 a）

　　　　　　　　　　注：/ = 強く発音される音節、× = 弱く発音される音節

　20世紀前半以降は、詩形にとらわれない詩も多く書かれています。改めて、自分が好きな詩や楽曲の英語の歌詞を分析してみると、新たな発見があるかもしれません。

# Session 11

Tennessee Williams, *A Streetcar Named Desire*

## ―会話の意図をつかみ取る―

### Pre-Reading

　話し言葉は、そのときの話し手の意図を直接的あるいは間接的に相手に伝えるものです。発言の内容や言い方は聞き手にさまざまな影響を与え、話し手は聞き手から予測どおりの応答を得ることもあれば、意外な反応を得てその結果思いもよらぬ発言をし、話が予期せぬ方向に進むこともあります。会話はキャッチボールのようなもので、その一連の流れによって、人間関係そのもののあり方が決定づけられることにもなります。

　この session では、アメリカの劇作家テネシー・ウィリアムズ（Tennessee Williams, 1911–83）の代表作、『欲望という名の電車』（*A Streetcar Named Desire*, 1947）から 2 つの場面を取り上げます。主人公である元女教師ブランチ（Blanche）と工場労働者のミッチ（Mitch）が、お互いの気持ちを探ろうとするかのように会話を交わしています。2 人がどのような表現を使っているかに注目し、そこに込められた意図を的確に読み取ることで、2 人の関係性が明確になってくるでしょう。そこから、読み手はその人物のキャラクターがどのようなものであるか、イメージを膨らませていくことができます。演出家になった気分で、戯曲を深く読んでみましょう。

### Reading Focus

1. 会話から 2 人の人間関係を読み取りましょう。
2. 登場人物のキャラクターが話し言葉を通してどのように形作られるのか、読んで体感しましょう。

11. Tennessee Williams, *A Streetcar Named Desire*

# Reading

<Text 1>

**BLANCHE**: Honey, you open the door while I take a last look at the sky. (*She leans on the porch rail. He opens the door and stands awkwardly behind her.*) I'm looking for the Pleiades, the Seven Sisters, but these girls are not out tonight. Oh, yes they are, there they are! God bless them! All in a bunch going home from their little bridge party. . . . Y' get the door open? Good boy! I guess you — want to go now . . . [5]
(*He shuffles and coughs a little.*)

**MITCH**: Can I — uh — kiss you — goodnight?

**BLANCHE**: Why do you always ask me if you may?

**MITCH**: I don't know whether you want me to or not.

**BLANCHE**: Why should you be so doubtful? [10]

**MITCH**: That night when we parked by the lake and I kissed you, you —

**BLANCHE**: Honey, it wasn't the kiss I objected to. I liked the kiss very much. It was the other little — familiarity — that I — felt obliged to — discourage. . . . I didn't resent it! Not a bit in the world! In fact, I was somewhat flattered that you — desired

---

[1] **you open the door:** Mitch に鍵の掛かった玄関のドアを開けてもらおうとしている。

[1–2] ***She leans on the porch rail***:「彼女は、玄関ポーチの手すりに寄りかかる」。括弧内のイタリック体の部分はト書きにあたる。

[3] **the Pleiades:** [plíːədìːz | pláiədìːz]「プレアデス星団（すばる星）」

[3] **the Seven Sisters:** プレアデス星団が 7 つ星であることから来る表現。

[4] **God bless them!:** 星を見つけてうれしい気持ちを表す。

[4] **All in a bunch going home from their little bridge party:** 7 つ星をトランプ遊びのパーティから帰る娘たちの一団にたとえている。

[5] **Y':** you. 疑問文で、本来なら Did you get the door open? となる。

[5] **I guess you — want to go now . . . :** dash (—) や ellipsis (. . .) を用いて、言い淀んでいる様子を表している。

[7] **kiss you — goodnight:**「kiss + 〜 (人) + goodnight」で「〜におやすみのキスをする」。goodbye を使うと「お別れのキスをする」となる。

[12] **it wasn't the kiss I objected to.:**「いやだったのは、そのキスではなかったの」。強調構文の類。

[12–13] **it was the other little — familiarity — that I — felt obliged to — discourage. . . . :**「とめなきゃって感じたのは、むしろあの...馴れ馴れしさ...のほうよ」。ここでの little は、familiarity に対する話者の嫌悪感を表している。

[14] **I was somewhat flattered that 〜 :**「〜だなんて、結構うれしかったの」

me! But, honey, you know as well as I do that a single girl, a girl alone in the world, has got to keep a firm hold on her emotions or she'll be lost!

**MITCH** (*solemnly*): Lost?

**BLANCHE**: I guess you are used to girls that like to be lost. The kind that get lost immediately, on the first date! [5]

**MITCH**: I like you to be exactly the way that you are, because in all my — experience — I have never known anyone like you.

(*Blanche looks at him gravely; then she bursts into laughter and then claps a hand to her mouth.*)

**MITCH**: Are you laughing at me? [10]

**BLANCHE**: No, honey. The lord and lady of the house have not yet returned, so come in. We'll have a night-cap. Let's leave the lights off. Shall we?

**MITCH**: You just — do what you want to.

(*Blanche precedes him into the kitchen. The outer wall of the building disappears and the interiors of the two rooms can be dimly seen.*) [15]

**BLANCHE** (*remaining in the first room*): The other room's more comfortable — go on in. This crashing around in the dark is my search for some liquor.

**MITCH**: You want a drink?

**BLANCHE**: I want *you* to have a drink! You have been so anxious and solemn all evening, and so have I; we have both been anxious and solemn and now for these few [20] last remaining moment of our lives together — I want to create — *joie de vivre*! I'm lighting a candle.

**MITCH**: That's good.

---

[2] **keep a firm hold on her emotions:** 一時の感情に流されて、惑わされないようにすること。
[2] **or she'll be lost:**「さもないと、おかしくなっちゃうわ」
[6] **the way that you are:**「今の君のまま」
[11] **The lord and lady of the house:** Blanche が身を寄せている妹夫婦の Stella と Stanley。
[12] **a night-cap:**「寝酒」
[14] **The outer wall of the building disappears:** 紗幕に描かれた家の壁が消え、舞台の奥が現れる。
[17] **This crashing around in the dark:** 明かりをつけていないため、暗がりの中であちこちぶつかっている。
[21] **joie de vivre:**「生の喜び」。joy of living のフランス語。気持ちを楽にして喜びを感じられるひとときを持ちたいと思っている。

11. Tennessee Williams, *A Streetcar Named Desire*

<Text 2>

**BLANCHE**: Had you forgotten your invitation to supper?

**MITCH**: I wasn't going to see you any more.

**BLANCHE**: Wait a minute. I can't hear what you're saying and you talk so little that when you do say something, I don't want to miss a single syllable of it.... What am I looking around here for? Oh, yes — liquor! We've had so much excitement around [5] here this evening that I *am* boxed out of my mind! (*She pretends suddenly to find the bottle. He draws his foot up on the bed and stares at her contemptuously.*) Here's something. Southern Comfort! What is that, I wonder?

**MITCH**: If you don't know, it must belong to Stan.

**BLANCHE**: Take your foot off the bed. It has a light cover on it. Of course you boys [10] don't notice things like that. I've done so much with this place since I've been here.

**MITCH**: I bet you have.

**BLANCHE**: You saw it before I came. Well, look at it now! This room is almost — dainty! I want to keep it that way. I wonder if this stuff ought to be mixed with something? Ummm, it's sweet, so sweet! It's terribly, terribly sweet! Why, it's a *liqueur*, [15] I believe! Yes, that's what it *is*, a liqueur! (*Mitch grunts.*) I'm afraid you won't like it, but try it, and maybe you will.

**MITCH**: I told you already I don't want none of his liquor and I mean it. You ought to

---

[1] **Had you forgotten your invitation to supper?:** この日、Mitch を夕食に招いていた。
[5] **We've had so much excitement:** 妹夫婦のけんかに引き続いて、妊娠していた妹が産気づき病院に向かうという慌しい夕べであった。
[6] **I *am* boxed out of my mind!:**「どうかしてしまっているの！」
[7] **He draws his foot up on the bed:** ベッドに腰掛けていたが、ここで片足を引きつけて、土足でベッドの上に足を置く。
[7] **contemptuously:**「さげすんだような目で」
[8] **Southern Comfort:** バーボンをベースとしたリキュール。桃と柑橘類の香りがあり、カクテルに使われる。
[9] **Stan:** 妹の夫である Stanley の愛称。
[10] **light cover:** やわらかな薄手の生地のベッド・カバー。
[14] **this stuff:** 先ほどから手にしている酒。この後、一口飲んで味を確認している。
[17] **maybe you will.:** ＝maybe you will like it.

lay off his liquor.  He says you been lapping it up all summer like a wild-cat!

**BLANCHE**: What a fantastic statement!  Fantastic of him to say it,  fantastic of you to repeat it!  I won't descend to the level of such cheap accusations to answer them, even!

**MITCH**: Huh.

**BLANCHE**: What's in your mind?  I see something in your eyes! [5]

**MITCH** (*getting up*): It's dark in here.

**BLANCHE**: I like it dark.  The dark is comforting to me.

**MITCH**: I don't think I ever seen you in the light. (*Blanche laughs breathlessly*) That's a fact!

**BLANCHE**: Is it? [10]

**MITCH**: I've never seen you in the afternoon.

**BLANCHE**: Whose fault is that?

**MITCH**: You never want to go out in the afternoon.

**BLANCHE**: Why, Mitch, you're at the plant in the afternoon!

**MITCH**: Not Sunday afternoon.  I've asked you to go out with me sometimes on Sun- [15] days but you always make an excuse.  You never want to go out till after six and then it's always some place that's not lighted much.

**BLANCHE**: There is some obscure meaning in this but I fail to catch it.

**MITCH**: What it means is I've never had a real good look at you, Blanche.

**BLANCHE**: What are you leading up to? [20]

**MITCH**: Let's turn the light on here.

**BLANCHE** (*fearfully*): Light?  Which light?  What for?

---

[1] **you been lapping it up:** = you have been lapping it up. 当時の労働者階級の英語では、have を省略する傾向にある。lap up はむさぼるように喜びを感じながら飲む様子を示す。

[1] **all summer:** この夏の間、ブランチはこの家に滞在していた。

[3] **I won't descend to the level of such cheap accusations to answer them, even!:** 下卑た話に付き合う気はないことを表現している。

[8] **I ever seen:** = I have ever seen.

[14] **you're at the plant:** 工場で働いている。

[18] **I fail to catch it.:**「おっしゃりたい意味がわからないわ」

[20] **leading up to:** lead up to で「話を持っていく」。

11. Tennessee Williams, *A Streetcar Named Desire*

**MITCH**: This one with the paper thing on it. (*He tears the paper lantern off the light bulb. She utters a frightened gasp.*)

**BLANCHE**: What did you do that for?

**MITCH**: So I can take a look at you good and plain!

**BLANCHE**: Of course you don't really mean to be insulting! [5]

**MITCH**: No, just realistic.

**BLANCHE**: I don't want realism.

**MITCH**: Naw, I guess not.

**BLANCHE**: I'll tell you what I want.

---

[1–2] ***He tears the paper lantern off the light bulb.:*** Mitch が以前に Blanche のために取り付けたちょうちんのようなランプシェードを、ここでは自らむしり取っている。

[4] **good and plain:** good and はその後ろの形容詞の意味を強める副詞的な役割を果たしている。

[8] **Naw, I guess not.:** ＝ No, I guess you don't want realism.

### Post-Reading

1. Text 1 の 49 頁 8 行目、"Why do you always ask me if you may?" と同 10 行目、"Why should you be so doubtful?" の Blanche の台詞はともに疑問詞から始まる疑問文ですが、発言の意図はどのようなものか説明しなさい。
2. Text 1 において、Blanche と Mitch のどちらがその関係性において主導権を握っているでしょうか。具体的に台詞やト書きに言及しながら説明しなさい。
3. Text 2 では、Text 1 での 2 人の関係がどのように変化しているか、具体的に台詞やト書きに言及しながら説明しなさい。
4. Text 1 と 2 を読んで、Blanche がどのような性格の持ち主で、どのような問題を抱えている女性であるか、考えてみましょう。
5. Text 2 の最後の台詞、"I'll tell you what I want." に続けて、戯曲では Blanche が自分の欲しいものを英語 1 語で示しています。どのような単語が適切か、自由な発想で考えてみましょう。

# Session 12

Benjamin Franklin, "Thirteen Virtues" and
"Poor Richard's Maxims"

## ―モットーを書く―

### Pre-Reading

　このsessionで取り上げるベンジャミン・フランクリン（Benjamin Franklin, 1706–90）は、アメリカン・ドリームの体現者として今でも尊敬を集めるアメリカの偉人です。独立宣言、対英講和条約、合衆国憲法という三大建国文書のすべてに署名しているアメリカ建国の祖であると同時に、無一文から自らの腕一本で大ビジネスマンへと立身出世を遂げたセルフ・メイド・マンでもあります。彼の『自叙伝』（*An Autobiography*, 執筆 1771–90, 出版 1818）の中で最も有名な「十三の美徳」（"Thirteen Virtues"）は、一見、古臭い道徳の押しつけに見えるかもしれませんが、実は、人間的に尊敬され、かつ「勝ち組」に入るための秘訣となっています。フランクリンは、「金持ち＝悪人」という古くからのイメージを覆し、世俗的成功は道徳的人格形成と相互補完的であると考えました。それぞれの徳目がビジネスでの成功にどうつながるのか、確認してみましょう。

　一方、フランクリンのブラック・ユーモアが存分に発揮されているのが「貧しいリチャードの格言」（"Poor Richard's Maxims"）です。これは、1732年創刊のフランクリンの手になる『貧しいリチャードの暦』に登場したものです。現在の情報誌的役割を備えたこの暦は、主な読者である農民や漁民のために日の出の時刻や潮の満ち引きに関する情報を盛り込んだほか、リチャード・ソーンダーズという当時の平均的アメリカ人が語る形で、さまざまな人生訓を掲載しました。Haste makes Waste（急がば回れ）や There are no Gains, without Pains（努力なくして獲得なし）など勤勉実直を説くものが多い中、このsessionでは皮肉とユーモアに溢れ、現代人も苦笑いしながら深く頷いてしまう人生訓を選びました。フランクリンの愉快な一面を味わいながら、読んでみましょう。「不完全で愚かな人間」に対するフランクリンの深い理解と愛情が見えてくるはずです。

## 12. Benjamin Franklin, "Thirteen Virtues" and "Poor Richard's Maxims"

**Reading Focus**

1. 本文は、18世紀アメリカのやや古めかしい文体で書かれています。現代英語ではどう表現するかを考えながら読んでみましょう。
2. 「十三の美徳」と「貧しいリチャードの格言」を読み比べながら、ベンジャミン・フランクリンとはいかなる人物かを考えてみましょう。

# Reading

**\<Text 1\>** From "Thirteen Virtues"

1. Temperance: Eat not to Dulness.  Drink not to Elevation.
2. Silence: Speak not but what may benefit others or your self.  Avoid trifling Conversation.
3. Order: Let all your Things have their Places.  Let each Part of your Business have its Time. [5]
4. Resolution: Resolve to perform what you ought.  Perform without fail what you resolve.
5. Frugality: Make no Expence but to do good to others or yourself: i.e. Waste nothing.
6. Industry: Lose no Time. — Be always employ'd in something useful. — Cut off all unnecessary Actions. — [10]
7. Sincerity: Use no hurtful Deceit.  Think innocently and justly; and, if you speak; speak accordingly.

---

[1] **eat not:** = do not eat. 古い英語の用法で、動詞の後ろに not を続けて否定形を作る。以下、同様の例が見られる。
[1] **to Dulness:** 「感覚が鈍るほどまでに、疲労困憊するほどまでに」。Dulness = Dullness. 以下、現在では大文字が使われないところで使われているのも古い英語であるため。
[1] **Elevation:** 上に持ち上げること。心を元気づけること。ここでは特に、アルコールで気分が高揚すること。cf. elevator.
[2] **but:** = except. 前置詞。
[9] **employ'd:** = employed.
[11] **Think innocently:**「他人に対して何の後ろめたさも感じることのないように物事を考えよ」。innocent には「無垢な、無邪気な」の意味もあるが、ここでは、「罪のない、悪意のない、無害な」の意味。
[12] **accordingly:** 前述のことに沿うように。

**&lt;Text 2&gt;**   From "Poor Richard's Maxims"

A. Where there's Marriage without Love, there will be Love without Marriage.

B. Fish & Visitors stink in 3 days.

C. There are three faithful friends, an old wife, an old dog, and ready money.

D. Keep your eyes wide open before marriage, half shut afterwards.

E. Eat to please thyself, but dress to please others. [5]

F. He that falls in love with himself, will have no Rivals.

G. At 20 years of age the Will reigns; at 30 the Wit; at 40 the Judgment.

H. One good Husband is worth two good Wives; for the scarcer things are the more they're valued.

I. Most fools think they are only ignorant. [10]

---

[5] **thyself:** yourself の古語。
[6] **He:** = Someone.
[8] **the scarcer ～ the more ～:**「～が乏しければ乏しいほど～である」

## Post-Reading

1. Text 1 の第2から第7までの徳目について、やや古めかしい英語で書かれている本文を、命令形や禁止表現（Don't＋動詞の原形）を使った現代版「成功の秘訣」として、わかりやすい現在の英語に書き換えなさい。
 〈例〉 1. Don't eat too much.  Don't drink too much.

2. フランクリンにならって、自分自身の「成功の秘訣」五箇条を英語で書いてみましょう。どのような成功を収めるための五箇条か（ビジネスマン、政治家、アスリートとしてなど）を明記してから始めましょう。

3. Text 2 の9項目それぞれについて、表面的な意味を確認したうえで、そこに込められたフランクリンらしいユーモアにあふれた物の見方とはどのようなものか、説明してみましょう。

4. Text 2 から好きな項目を3つ選び、単語を適宜入れ替えて、趣旨の違った人生訓を作ってみましょう。

# Session 13

Tim O'Brien, "Ambush"

## ―事実と虚構の狭間を読む―

### Pre-Reading

　Session 6 と Session 7 で見たとおり、自分についての語りの文体は、文学としての物語に近い構造を持っています。とすると、自伝と「私」語りの小説をわけるものは何でしょうか？　事実を描いているか、虚構の物語か、それで線引きができればいいのですが、どうもそう話は簡単ではありません。自分のことを語る際、つねに事実を語るとは限らないからです。自分の過去を語る場合、単なる記憶違いによって事実とは違うことを話すこともありますし、事実を脚色することもあります。あるいは、事実だけを語っては都合が悪い場合、ところどころで虚構を差し挟むこともあります。そして、その語りが格調高い文体でなされた場合、もはや日常的な語りと文学とをわける線があるのかどうかもわからなくなってきます。

　この session では、どこまでが事実で、どこまでが虚構であるかわからない、あるいはそれを論じることにあまり意味のない文章を読んでみましょう。出典は、Tim O'Brien というアメリカ人作家の『本当の戦争の話をしよう』(*The Things They Carried*, 1990) という短編集です。作者自身が体験したヴェトナム戦争に材を取った作品であり、作者と同名の Tim O'Brien なる語り手が語りを務めますが、これは作者本人の回想録ではなく、あくまで 1 つのお話として読むべきものです。

## ⊕ Reading Focus ⊕

1. この物語は、語り手が娘との関係を語る冒頭の部分と、娘を仮想の聞き手として戦争の体験を語る部分と、大きく2つに分かれます。その文体の違いに注意しながら読んでみましょう。
2. 自分が語り手の娘になったと仮定して物語を読んでみましょう。どのような印象を受けるでしょうか？

# Reading

When she was nine, my daughter Kathleen asked if I had ever killed anyone. She knew about the war; she knew I'd been a soldier. 'You keep writing these war stories,' she said, 'so I guess you must've killed somebody.' It was a difficult moment, but I did what seemed right, which was to say, 'Of course not,' and then to take her unto my lap and hold her for a while. Someday, I hope, she'll ask again. But here I want to pretend [5] she's a grown-up. I want to tell her exactly what happened, or what I remember happening, and then I want to say to her that as a little girl she was absolutely right. This is why I keep writing war stories:

He was a short, slender young man of about twenty. I was afraid of him — afraid of something — as he passed me on the trail I threw a grenade that exploded at this feet and [10] killed him.

Or to go back:

Shortly after midnight we moved into the ambush site outside My Khe. The whole

---

[3] **I guess you must've killed somebody:**「お父さんはきっと誰かを殺したことがあるんでしょう」。must've = must have.
[5–6] **here I want to pretend she's a grown-up:**「ここでは、娘が大きくなったと仮定して話をしよう」。pretend (that) ... は、「～のふりをする、～ということを装う」の意。
[10] **grenade:**「手榴弾」
[12] **Or to go back:**「もう一度最初から話すと、もとへ」
[13] **ambush site:**「待ち伏せ地点」
[13] **My Khe:** 地名。[miːkeɪ] と読む。

13. Tim O'Brien, "Ambush"

platoon was there, spread out in the dense brush along the trail, and for five hours nothing at all happened. We were working in two-man teams — one man on guard while the other slept, switching off every two hours — and I remember it was still dark when Kiowa shook me awake for the final watch. The night was foggy and hot. For the first few moments I felt lost, not sure about directions, groping for my helmet and weapon. I [5] reached out and found three grenades and lined them up in front of me; the pins had already been straightened for quick throwing. And then for maybe half an hour I kneeled there and waited. Very gradually, in tiny silvers, dawn began to break through the fog, and from my position in the brush I could see ten or fifteen meters up the trail. The mosquitoes were fierce. I remember slapping at them, wondering if I should wake up Kiowa [10] and ask for some repellent, then thinking it was a bad idea, then looking up and seeing the young man come out of the fog. He wore black clothing and rubber sandals and a gray ammunition belt. His shoulders were slightly stooped, his head cocked to the side as if listening for something. He seemed at ease. He carried his weapon in one hand, muzzle down, moving without any hurry up the center of the trail. There was no sound [15] at all — none that I can remember. In a way, it seemed, he was part of the morning fog, or my own imagination, but there was also the reality of what was happening in my stomach. I had already pulled the pin on a grenade. I had come up to a crouch. It was entirely automatic. I did not hate the young man; I did not see him as the enemy; I did not ponder issues of morality or politics or military duty. I crouched and kept my head [20] low. I tried to swallow whatever was rising from my stomach, which tasted like lemonade, something fruity and sour. I was terrified. There were no thoughts about killing.

---

[1] **platoon:**「小隊」
[2] **in two-man teams:**「2人1組になって」。この two-man のように基数詞と名詞をハイフンでつないで1つの形容詞として用いる場合、名詞が複数形にならないことに注意。ex. five-year project.
[3–4] **Kiowa:** 人の名前。[kíːəwɑː] と読む。
[6–7] **the pins had already been straightened for quick throwing:**「すぐに投げられるように、手榴弾の安全ピンが（抜きやすいように）まっすぐになっていた」
[8] **in tiny silvers:** 幾筋もの銀色の日の光が射している様を表している。
[11] **repellent:**「防虫剤」。本来は、虫を「追い払う」（repel）ものの意。
[13] **ammunition belt:**「弾薬帯」
[15] **muzzle down:**「銃口を下げた状態で」
[18] **I had come up to a crouch:**「私は立ち上がって身をかがめていた」

The grenade was to make him go away — just evaporate — and I leaned back and felt my mind go empty and then felt it fill up again. I had already thrown the grenade before telling myself to throw it. The brush was thick and I had to lob it high, not aiming, and I remember the grenade seeming to freeze above me for an instant, as if a camera had clicked, and I remember ducking down and holding my breath and seeing little wisps of fog rise from the earth. The grenade bounced once and rolled across the trail. I did not hear it, but there must've been a sound, because the young man dropped his weapon and began to run, just two or three quick steps, then he hesitated, swiveling to his right, and he glanced down at the grenade and tried to cover his head but never did. It occurred to me then that he was about to die. I wanted to warn him. The grenade made a popping noise — not soft but not loud either — not what I'd expected — and there was a puff of dust and smoke — a small white puff — and the young man seemed to jerk upward as if pulled by invisible wires. He fell on his back. His rubber sandals had been blown off. There was no wind. He lay at the center of the trail, his right leg bent beneath him, his one eye shut, his other eye a huge star-shaped hole.

It was not a matter of live or die. There was no real peril. Almost certainly the young man would have passed by. And it will always be that way.

Later, I remember, Kiowa tried to tell me that the man would've died anyway. He told me that it was a good kill, that I was a soldier and this was a war, that I should shape up and stop staring and ask myself what the dead man would've done if things were reversed.

None of it mattered. The words seemed far too complicated. All I could do was gape at the fact of the young man's body.

Even now I haven't finished sorting it out. Sometimes I forgive myself, other times I

---

[1] **evaporate:**「(蒸発するように) 消えてなくなる」
[3] **lob it high:**「ポーンと高く放る」
[5–6] **wisps of fog rise from the earth:**「地面から煙が立ち上った」。手榴弾が地面に当たって土煙を上げたのである。
[8] **swiveling to his right:**「右に体を回転させて」。分詞構文。
[19] **it was a good kill:**「(どうせ死ぬんだから) うまく死なせてやったよ」
[24] **I haven't finished sorting it out:**「整理し終えていない」。このときの出来事を自分のなかできちんと納得がいく形で理解できていないということ。sort out は「解決する、整理する」の意。

don't. In the ordinary hours of life I try not to dwell on it, but now and then, when I'm reading a newspaper or just sitting alone in a room, I'll look up and see the young man coming out of the morning fog. I'll watch him walk toward me, his shoulders slightly stooped, his head cocked to the side, and he'll pass within a few yards of me and suddenly smile at some secret thought and then continue up the trail to where it bends back into the fog. [5]

---

[1] **dwell on . . .** :「〜についてくよくよ考える」

## Post-Reading

1. 語り手は、なぜ第3パラグラフで 'Or to go back'（58頁12行目）と言って、最初から語り直したのかを考えてみましょう。
2. 語り手は、戦場で敵の兵隊に対してどのような感情を抱きましたか。テキストに即して答えなさい。
3. 緊迫した状況下で語り手が体験した知覚の混乱を示す表現をできるだけ多く抜き出してみましょう。

# Session 14

Lori Peikoff, "Table for Two"

## —逸話を語る—

### Pre-Reading

　いま、多くの企業が社員に「コミュニケーション能力」を求めています。文筆業とは縁もゆかりもない人にも、自分の言葉に目をとめ耳を傾けてもらう技術が必要になっているのです。これほど広く一般の人に、語りのテクニックが求められる時代はありませんでした。しかし、そんな時代の要請にあった言葉の技術を磨くためには、どうしたらよいのでしょう。

　人はだれでも、だれかに語らずにはいられない、とっておきの逸話というものをひとつやふたつは持っているものです。まずはそのような、中味の面白さには自信が持てる逸話を、うまく伝える練習からはじめてみてはどうでしょうか。

　ここでは、アメリカの現代作家ポール・オースター（Paul Auster, 1947– ）がアメリカのラジオ番組でリスナーに呼びかけて集めた「作り話のような実話」のひとつを読み、「作り話のよう」とはどういうことなのかを考え、人に目をとめ耳を傾けてもらえる語り方のヒントをつかみましょう。

### Reading Focus

　この作品では、イギリス小説の名作が若い男女の出会いの小道具として効果的に用いられています。そのような小説が小道具として使われたことによって、この物語にどのようなふくらみが生まれているかについて考えてみましょう。

14. Lori Peikoff, "Table for Two"

# Reading

In 1947 my mother, Deborah, was a twenty-one-year-old student at New York University, majoring in English literature. She was beautiful — fiery yet introspective — with a great passion for books and ideas. She read voraciously and hoped one day to become a writer.

My father, Joseph, was an aspiring painter who supported himself by teaching art at [5] a junior high school on the West Side. On Saturdays he would paint all day, either at home or in Central Park, and treat himself to a meal out. On the Saturday night in question, he chose a neighborhood restaurant called the Milky Way.

The Milky Way happened to be my mother's favorite restaurant, and that Saturday, after studying throughout the morning and early afternoon, she went there for dinner, [10] carrying along a used copy of Dickens's *Great Expectations*. The restaurant was crowded, and she was given the last table. She settled in for an evening of goulash, red wine, and Dickens — and quickly lost touch of what was going on around her.

Within half an hour, the restaurant was standing-room-only. The frazzled hostess came over and asked my mother if she would be willing to share her table with someone [15] else. Barely glancing up from her book, my mother agreed.

"A tragic life for poor dear Pip," my father said when he saw the tattered cover of *Great*

---

[1–2] **New York University:** 芸術家の街といわれるグリニッジヴィレッジ地区に校舎が点在する私立大学。
[3] **one day:**「いつの日か」。直前の hoped ではなく、うしろの become を修飾する副詞句。
[6] **West Side:** セントラルパーク西側の住宅地。現在は高額所得者の居住区だが、1947 年当時はむしろ低所得者層の居住区であった。
[7] **treat himself to a meal out:**「ちょっと奮発して外食をする」
[7–8] **in question:**「(この話でとりあげることになる) 問題の」
[8] **the Milky Way:** ここでは店の名前だが、「天の川、銀河」の意味を持った店名をさり気なく入れることで、物語に彩りを与えている。
[11] **a used copy:**「(1 冊の) 古本」
[11] **Dickens:** *Oliver Twist* (1837–38), *A Christmas Carol* (1843), *David Copperfield* (1849–50), *A Tale of Two Cities* (1859), そして本文中に登場する *Great Expectations* (1860–61) などの名作で知られる、イギリスを代表する小説家。session 15 も参照のこと。
[12] **goulash:**「グーラーシュ」。中欧ハンガリーのビーフシチュー。辛みのない唐辛子 (パプリカ) のパウダーが入っているのが特徴。

*Expectations*. My mother looked up at him, and at that moment, she recalls, she saw something strangely familiar in his eyes. Years later, when I begged her to tell me the story one more time, she sighed sweetly and said, "I saw myself in his eyes."

My father, entirely captivated by the presence before him, swears to this day that he heard a voice inside his head. "She is your destiny," the voice said, and immediately after that he felt a tingling sensation that ran from the tips of his toes to the crown of his head. Whatever it was that my parents saw or heard or felt that night, they both understood that something miraculous had happened.

Like two old friends catching up after a long absence from one another, they talked for hours. Later on, when the evening was over, my mother wrote her telephone number on the inside cover of *Great Expectations* and gave the book to my father. He said goodbye to her, gently kissing her on the forehead, and then they walked off in opposite directions into the night.

Neither one of them was able to sleep. Even after she closed her eyes, my mother could see only one thing: my father's face. And my father, who could not stop thinking about her, stayed up all night painting my mother's portrait.

The next day, Sunday, he traveled out to Brooklyn to visit his parents. He brought along the book to read on the subway, but he was exhausted after his sleepless night and started feeling drowsy after just a few paragraphs. So he slipped the book into the pocket of his coat — which he had put on the seat next to him — and closed his eyes. He didn't wake until the train stopped at Brighton Beach, at the far edge of Brooklyn.

The train was deserted by then, and when he opened his eyes and reached for his things, the coat was no longer there. Someone had stolen it, and because the book was in the pocket, the book was gone, too. Which meant that my mother's telephone number was also gone. In desperation, he began to search the train, looking under every seat,

---

[1–2] **at that moment, she recalls, she saw . . . :**「そのとき母は（本人の述懐によれば）、〜を見たという」
[4] **to this day:**「きょうに至るまで、いまでも同じことを」
[6–7] **the crown of his head:**「あたまのてっぺん」
[17] **Brooklyn:** マンハッタンとイーストリバーをへだてて南東にある住宅地。
[21] **Brighton Beach:** 地下鉄B線の終点。
[22] **The train was deserted:**「乗客がすべて降りたあとだった」

not only in his car but in the cars on either side of him. In his excitement over meeting Deborah, Joseph had foolishly neglected to find out her last name. The telephone number was his only link to her.

The call my mother was expecting never came. My father went looking for her several times at the NYU English Department, but he could never find her. Destiny had betrayed them both. What had seemed inevitable that first night in the restaurant was apparently not meant to be.

That summer, they both headed for Europe. My mother went to England to take literature courses at Oxford, and my father went to Paris to paint. In late July, with a three-day break in her studies my mother flew to Paris, determined to absorb as much culture as she possibly could in seventy-two hours. She carried along a new copy of *Great Expectations* on the trip. After the sad business with my father, she hadn't had the heart to read it, but now, as she sat down in a crowded restaurant after a long day of sight-seeing, she opened it to the first page and started thinking about him again.

After reading a few sentences, she was interrupted by a maître d' who asked her, first in French, then in broken English, if she wouldn't mind sharing her table. She agreed and then returned to her reading. A moment later, she heard a familiar voice.

"A tragic life for poor dear Pip," the voice said, and then she looked up, and there he was again.

---

[1] **his car:**「彼が乗っていた車両」
[5] **NYU:** New York University の通称。[en waɪ júː] と読む。
[6–7] **was apparently not meant to be:**「明らかに運命的なものではなかったらしい」
[12] **the sad business:**「悲しいできごと」
[15] **maître d':** フロアを取り仕切り、客をふさわしい席に案内する係。

## Post-Reading

1. 各段落に 1 行の英語のタイトルをつけ、一覧表にして物語の全体の流れを見渡してみましょう。
2. Joseph が 2 回言ったセリフに下線をひき、その意味を考えてみましょう。
3. Deborah が読んでいた本を、Dickens の *Great Expectations* 以外のものに置き換えると、この話にどのような違いが生じるか考えてみましょう。
4. この物語の語り手は、ディケンズの小説を効果的に用いているだけでなく、いろいろな工夫をしながら読者の興味を引きつけています。そのような工夫をいくつか挙げてみましょう。たとえば、語り手のお父さんとお母さんそれぞれの生活の描写や、彼らの 1 回目の出会いと 2 回目の出会いの語り方にどのような類似点、相違点があるでしょうか。

---

### ● Column 5 ●

#### 文学的素養は究極のコミュニケーション・ツール

　Pre-Reading では、「とっておきの逸話」を語るという形でのコミュニケーションの図り方に触れましたが、この session で読んだ物語自体、見事なコミュニケーションのあり方を描いたものだと言えないでしょうか。何しろ、『大いなる遺産』に関するやり取りが、恋愛に、さらには結婚に発展したのですから、これぞ究極のコミュニケーションだと言うこともできます。もしも語り手のお父さんがディケンズなど読んだこともなく、ただ相席をめぐる簡単な挨拶の言葉を言って席についたとしたら、この素敵な物語は生まれなかったかもしれません。そうなると、そもそもこの語り手が生まれていませんよね。あるいは、単に「ディケンズを読んでいらっしゃるのですか」ではなく、きちんと物語を知っていて、「ピップがあまりにもかわいそうですよね」という言い方をしたのが効いたのではないでしょうか。

　たしかに文学作品を読んで英語を身につけても、それがすぐさま効き目を現すことはあまりありません。TOEIC や TOEFL の点数が目覚ましく上がることもなければ（ただ英語力認定試験の点数を上げたいなら、当然ながら試験対策をするのが一番です）、買い物が上手になるわけでもありません。しかしながら、文学的素養はあとになってじんわりと効いてきます。そして、それを身につけた人の人となりを作っていく重要な要素になります。目先の実用だけを目指すのでなく、のちのち教養として輝きを放つような英語を身につけるためにも、時おり文学の英語を読むようにしてください。

# Session 15

Charles Dickens, *Great Expectations*

## ―名作の原文を読む―

## Pre-Reading

　このsessionでは、文学を用いた英語の勉強の締めくくりとして、前のsessionにも出てくる文豪チャールズ・ディケンズ（Charles Dickens, 1812–70）の『大いなる遺産』（*Great Expectations*, 1860–61）の原文を見ることにします。

　『大いなる遺産』は、鍛冶屋を営む姉夫婦に育てられた孤児のピップ（Pip）が、匿名の後援者からの経済的援助を受けて紳士としての教育を受けた末、その後援者をめぐる事件に巻き込まれていく物語です。物語を織り成す主要な筋の一本として、謎の資産家ミス・ハヴィシャム（Miss Havisham）の養女エステラ（Estella）に対するピップの片想いがあります。男性を嫌悪するミス・ハヴィシャムの教えを忠実に守るエステラは、彼の求愛を冷たく振り切ってドラムル（Drummle）なる男と結婚しますが、虐待を受けたあげくに離婚、人生の厳しさを学んで人間としての優しさを身につけ、長年の歳月を経てピップと再会します。

　ところで、この物語には2つの結末が存在します。1つは、もともとディケンズが考えていた結末。そしてもう1つは、草稿を読んだ小説家エドワード・ブルワー＝リットン（Edward Bulwer-Lytton, 1803–73）の強い勧めによって書いた別の結末であり、それが最終的に発表されたものです。Text 1, Text 2のいずれが元の結末で、いずれが最終的に完成した作品の結末となったかは、あえて伏せてあります。

## Reading Focus

2つの結末を読み比べてみましょう。

# Reading

<Text 1>

 I had heard of her as leading a most unhappy life, and as being separated from her husband who had used her with great cruelty, and who had become quite renowned as a compound of pride, brutality and meanness. I had heard of the death of her husband (from an accident consequent on ill-treating a horse), and of her being married again to a Shropshire doctor, who, against his interest, had once very manfully interposed, on [5] an occasion when he was in professional attendance on Mr. Drummle, and had witnessed some outrageous treatment of her. I had heard that the Shropshire doctor was not rich, and that they lived on her own personal fortune. I was in England again — in London, and walking along Piccadilly with little Pip — when a servant came running after me to ask would I step back to a lady in a carriage who wished to speak to me. It was a little [10] pony carriage, which the lady was driving; and the lady and I looked sadly enough on one another. 'I am greatly changed, I know; but I thought you would like to shake hands with Estella too, Pip. Lift up that pretty child and let me kiss it!' (She supposed the child, I think, to be my child.) I was very glad afterwards to have had the interview; for, in her face and in her voice, and in her touch, she gave me the assurance, that suffering [15] had been stronger than Miss Havisham's teaching, and had given her a heart to understand what my heart used to be.

---

[1] **I had heard of her as . . . :**「彼女が〜であるとの噂を聞いていた」
[2] **used:** = treated.
[2–3] **renowned as a compound of pride, brutality, and meanness:**「高慢で残忍で卑劣な人間として悪名高い」。compound は「合体したもの」の意。
[5] **Shropshire doctor:**「シュロップシャーに住む医者」。Shropshire はイングランド中西部の州。
[5] **against his interest:**「利に反して、自分の得にはならないのに」
[5] **manfully interposed:** Estella が夫の虐待を受けているときに、「男らしく割って入った」ということ。
[9] **Piccadilly:** ロンドンにある大通り。
[9] **little Pip:** 鍛冶屋を営む Pip の義兄 Joe と、Pip の幼なじみで Joe の再婚相手である Biddy の間に生まれた子供。
[9] **when . . . :**「そのとき〜した」
[10] **ask would I step back:** = ask if I would step back.

## 15. Charles Dickens, *Great Expectations*

**<Text 2>**

　I had heard of her as leading a most unhappy life, and as being separated from her husband, who had used her with great cruelty, and who had become quite renowned as a compound of pride, avarice, brutality, and meanness. And I had heard of the death of her husband, from an accident consequent on his ill-treatment of a horse. This release had befallen her some two years before; for anything I knew, she was married again.　[5]

　The early dinner-hour at Joe's left me abundance of time, without hurrying my talk with Biddy, to walk over to the old spot before dark. But, what with loitering on the way, to look at old objects and to think of old times, the day had quite declined when I came to the place.

　There was no house now, no brewery, no building whatever left, but the wall of the [10] old garden. The cleared space had been enclosed with a rough fence, and looking over it, I saw that some of the old ivy had struck root anew, and was growing green on low quiet mounds of ruin. A gate in the fence standing ajar, I pushed it open and went in.

　A cold silvery mist had veiled the afternoon, and the moon was not yet up to scatter it. But the stars were shining beyond the mist, and the moon was coming, and the evening [15] was not dark. I could trace out where every part of the old house had been, and where the brewery had been, and where the gates, and where the casks. I had done so, and was looking along the desolate garden-walk, when I beheld a solitary figure in it.

　The figure showed itself aware of me as I advanced. It had been moving towards me, but it stood still. As I drew nearer, I saw it to be the figure of a woman. As I drew [20] nearer yet, it was about to turn away, when it stopped, and let me come up with it. Then, it faltered as if much surprised, and uttered my name, and I cried out:

---

[4] **This release:** 夫の死により Estella が解放されたこと。
[5] **for anything I knew:**「よくは知らないが」
[7] **what with loitering on the way:**「途中、道草を食ったこともあって」。what with . . . and what with 〜「...やら〜やらで」の形で使われることも多い。
[10] **There was . . . no building whatever left:**「〜も、〜も、建物一つまったく残っていなかった」。ここでの whatever は、no をともなう名詞のうしろについて否定を強調する形容詞として用いられている。
[13] **A gate in the fence standing ajar:**「垣根にある門が空いていたので」。独立分詞構文。
[21] **come up with . . . :**「〜に追いつく」

'Estella!'

'I am greatly changed. I wonder you know me.'

The freshness of her beauty was indeed gone, but its indescribable majesty and its indescribable charm remained. Those attractions in it I had seen before; what I had never seen before was the saddened softened light of the once proud eyes; what I had never felt before was the friendly touch of the once insensible hand. [5]

We sat down on a bench that was near, and I said, 'After so many years, it is strange that we should thus meet again, Estella, here where our first meeting was! Do you often come back?'

'I have never been here since.' [10]

'Nor I.'

The moon began to rise, and I thought of the placid look at the white ceiling, which had passed away. The moon began to rise, and I thought of the pressure on my hand when I had spoken the last words he had heard on earth.

Estella was the next to break the silence that ensued between us. [15]

'I have very often hoped and intended to come back, but have been prevented by many circumstances. Poor, poor old place!'

The silvery mist was touched with the first rays of the moonlight, and the same rays touched the tears that dropped from her eyes. Not knowing that I saw them, and setting herself to get the better of them, she said quietly: [20]

'Were you wondering, as you walked along, how it came to be left in this condition?'

---

[6] **the friendly touch of the once insensible hand:** かつては握手をしてもまるで無反応だったのに、そこに温もりが感じられるようになったということ。

[8] **should:** 驚きや意外の気持ちを表す主節に続く名詞節の中で用いられる should。「〜すべき」という意味はない。次ページの 19 行目の should も同じ。

[12-14] **The moon began to rise, and I thought of the placid look at the white ceiling, which had passed away. The moon began to rise, and I thought of the pressure on my hand when I had spoken the last words he had heard on earth.:** この一段落には、Pip が幼少時に助けた脱獄囚で、のちに彼の匿名の後援者となる Magwitch の臨終の場面（第 56 章）への言及がある。the placid look at the white ceiling は、Magwitch が死の床で静かに白い天井を見上げている様子を、また the pressure on my hand when I had spoken the last words he had heard on earth は、死の床で Pip から Estella の消息を聞いた彼の反応を指している。なんと Estella は、Magwitch の実の娘だったのである。

[20] **get the better of them:**「涙を止める」。them = the tears. get the better of 〜 で「〜に打ち勝つ」。

## 15. Charles Dickens, *Great Expectations*

'Yes, Estella.'

'The ground belongs to me. It is the only possession I have not relinquished. Everything else has gone from me, little by little, but I have kept this. It was the subject of the only determined resistance I made in all the wretched years.'

'Is it to be built on?' [5]

'At last it is. I came here to take leave of it before its change. And you,' she said, in a voice of touching interest to a wanderer, 'you live abroad still.'

'Still.'

'And do well, I am sure?'

'I work pretty hard for a sufficient living, and therefore — Yes, I do well!' [10]

'I have often thought of you,' said Estella.

'Have you?'

'Of late, very often. There was a long hard time when I kept far from me the remembrance of what I had thrown away when I was quite ignorant of its worth. But, since my duty has not been incompatible with the admission of that remembrance, I have given it [15] a place in my heart.'

'You have always held your place in *my* heart,' I answered.

And we were silent again until she spoke.

'I little thought,' said Estella, 'that I should take leave of you in taking leave of this spot. I am very glad to do so.' [20]

'Glad to part again, Estella? To me parting is a painful thing. To me, the remembrance of our last parting has been ever mournful and painful.'

---

[3-4] **the only determined resistance:** 他の財産は少しずつ処分せざるを得なかったけれども、この土地だけは断固として処分に抵抗してきたということ。

[6-7] **in a voice of touching interest to a wanderer:**「放浪の身にはじんとくるような、思いやりのある声で」。昔の Estella とは違い、ただの社交辞令ではなくて、本当に自分に興味を持って質問をしてきたということ。それが Pip にとって touching（じんとくる）ものだったのである。

[15-16] **I have given it a place in my heart:**「それを心の中に大事にしまっておくようにした」。it「それ」とは、その前の the remembrance of what I had thrown away when I was quite ignorant of its worth と that remembrance を指している。すなわち、Pip との思い出も含め、その価値もわからずにいったんは捨ててしまった昔の思い出のこと。

'But you said to me,' returned Estella, very earnestly, '"God bless you, God forgive you!" And if you could say that to me then, you will not hesitate to say that to me now — now, when suffering has been stronger than all other teaching, and has taught me to understand what your heart used to be. I have been bent and broken, but — I hope — into a better shape. Be as considerate and good to me as you were, and tell me we are friends.' [5]

'We are friends,' said I, rising and bending over her, as she rose from the bench.

'And will continue friends apart,' said Estella.

I took her hand in mine, and we went out of the ruined place; and, as the morning mists had risen long ago when I first left the forge, so, the evening mists were rising now, [10] and in all the broad expanse of tranquil light they showed to me, I saw no shadow of another parting from her.

---

[1] **God bless you, God forgive you!:** かつて Pip が、自分の求愛を拒んで Drummle との結婚を決めた Estella との別れ際、彼女に向かって思わず叫んだ言葉。

## Post-Reading

1. 2つの結末を比べ、どこがどのように違っているかを具体的に説明しなさい。
2. どちらの結末が自分の好みにあっているかを、理由を添えて述べなさい。

# Appendix

ここでは、session には含められなかった作品で、学習に役立ててもらえる興味深いテクストを掲載しています。さまざまな作品に親しむ機会を増やすきっかけとしてください。

## 1. 言葉遊びを体験する

### ● Tongue Twisters

<Text 1>

She sells sea shells by the seashore.
The shells she sells are surely seashells.
So if she sells shells on the seashore,
I'm sure she sells seashore shells.

<Text 2>

A flea and a fly flew up in a flue.
Said the flea, 'Let us fly!'
Said the fly, 'Let us flee!'
So they flew through a flaw in the flue.

<Text 3>

Of all the felt I ever felt,
I never felt a piece of felt
Which felt as fine as that felt felt,
When first I felt that felt hat's felt.

---

* グループの中でだれか一人を選び出すときの歌。

### ● Nursery Rhymes

<Text 1>　鬼決め歌*

Eeny, meeny, miny, moe,
Catch a tiger by the toe.
If he hollers let him go,
Eeny, meeny, miny, moe.

<Text 2>　鬼決め歌

Hickory, dickory, dock,
The mouse ran up the clock.
The clock struck one,
The mouse ran down,
Hickory, dickory, dock.

<Text 3>　ナンセンス詩

Hey diddle diddle,
The cat and the fiddle,
The cow jumped over the moon;
The little dog laughed
To see such sport,
And the dish ran away with the spoon.

**<Text 4>** 遊び歌

London Bridge is broken down,[†]
Broken down, broken down,
London Bridge is broken down,
　My fair lady.

Built it up with wood and clay,
Wood and clay, wood and clay,
Built it up with wood and clay,
　My fair lady.

Wood and clay will wash away,
Wash away, wash away,
Wood and clay will wash away,
　My fair lady.

Built it up with bricks and mortar,
Bricks and mortar, bricks and mortar,
Built it up with bricks and mortar,
　My fair lady.

Bricks and mortar will not stay,
Will not stay, will not stay,
Bricks and mortar will not stay,
　My fair lady.

Built it up with iron and steel,
Iron and steel, iron and steel,
Built it up with iron and steel,
　My fair lady.

Iron and steel will bend and bow,
Bend and bow, bend and bow,
Iron and steel will bend and bow,
　My fair lady.

Built it up with silver and gold,
Silver and gold, silver and gold,
Built it up with silver and gold,
　My fair lady.

Silver and gold will be stolen away,
Stolen away, stolen away,
Silver and gold will be stolen away,
　My fair lady.

Set a man to watch all night,
Watch all night, watch all night,
Set a man to watch all night,
　My fair lady.

Suppose the man should fall asleep,
Fall asleep, fall asleep,
Suppose the man should fall asleep,
　My fair lady.

---

[†] 日本ではアメリカ経由で入ってきた 'London Bridge is falling down,' が一般に知られているが、もともとの歌では 'broken' となっている。

Give him a pipe to smoke all night,
Smoke all night, smoke all night,
Give him a pipe to smoke all night,
   My fair lady

## ● Limericks

### &lt;Text 1&gt;

A circus performer named Brian
Once smiled as he rode on a lion.
   They came back from the ride,
   But with Brian inside,
And the smile on the face of the lion.

### &lt;Text 2&gt;

There was a young lady who tried
A diet of apples and died.
   The unfortunate miss
   Really perished of this:
Too much cider inside her inside.

### &lt;Text 3&gt;

There's a clever old miser who tries
Every method to e-con-o-mise.
   He said with a wink,
   'I save gallons of ink
By simply not dotting my i's.'

# 2. 芭蕉の句をさまざまな英訳で味わう

**<Text 1>** 古池や 蛙(かはづ)飛込(とびこ)む水のをと

**A.** Translated by Asataro Miyamori

The ancient pond!
A frog plunged — splash!

**B.** Translated by Yone Noguchi

The old pond!
A frog leapt into —
List, the water sound!

**C.** Translated by Hidesaburo Saito

Old garden lake!
　　The frog thy depth doth seek,
　　　　And sleeping echoes wake.

**<Text 2>** 夏草(なつくさ)や 兵(つはもの)どもが夢の跡

**A.** Translated by Asataro Miyamori

Ah, summer grasses wave!
The warriors' brave deeds were a dream!

**B.** Translated by Inazo Nitobe

The summer grass!
'Tis all that's left
Of ancient warriors' dreams.

**C.** Translated by William N. Porter

　　Asleep within the grave
The soldiers dream, and overhead
　　The summer grasses wave.

# 3. 英詩を楽しむ

## ●やさしい詩

**\<Text 1\>**　Gertrude Stein, 'I Am Rose' (1939)

I am Rose my eyes are blue

I am Rose and who are you?

I am Rose and when I sing

I am Rose like anything.

**\<Text 2\>**　Gerard Manley Hopkins, 'In the Staring Darkness' (執筆 1866)

In the staring darkness

I can hear the harshness

Of the cold wind blowing.

I am warmly clad,

And I'm very glad

That I've got a home.

## ●愛をめぐって

**\<Text 1\>**　Emily Dickinson, 'To Wait an Hour — is long' (執筆 1864)

To wait an Hour — is long —

If Love be just beyond —

To wait Eternity — is short —

If Love reward the end —

**\<Text 2\>**　Christina G. Rossetti, 'A Birthday' (1861)

My heart is like a singing bird

　　Whose nest is in a watered shoot;

My heart is like an apple tree

　　Whose boughs are bent with thickset fruit;

My heart is like a rainbow shell

That paddles in a halcyon sea;
My heart is gladder than all these
　　Because my love is come to me.

Raise me a dais of silk and down;
　　Hang it with vair and purple dyes;
Carve it in doves and pomegranates,
　　And peacocks with a hundred eyes;
Work it in gold and silver grapes,
　　In leaves and silver fleurs-de-lys;
Because the birthday of my life
　　Is come, my love is come to me.

### &lt;Text 3&gt;　John Clare, 'Love's Pains' (執筆 1844)

#### 1
This love, I canna' bear it,
It cheats me night and day;
This love, I canna' wear it,
It takes my peace away.

#### 2
This love, wa' once a flower;
But now it is a thorn, —
The joy o' evening hour,
Turn'd to a pain e're morn.

#### 3
This love, it wa' a bud,
And a secret known to me;
Like a flower within a wood;
Like a nest within a tree.

#### 4
This love, wrong understood,
Oft' turned my joy to pain;
I tried to throw away the bud,
But the blossom would remain.

## ●生を考える

**<Text 1>** Stephen Crane, 'In the Desert' (1895)

In the desert
I saw a creature, naked, bestial,
Who, squatting upon the ground,
Held his heart in his hands,
And ate of it.
I said: 'Is it good, friend?'
'It is bitter — bitter,' he answered;
'But I like it
Because it is bitter,
And because it is my heart.'

**<Text 2>** A. E. Housman, 'When I was one-and-twenty' (1896)

When I was one-and-twenty
   I heard a wise man say,
'Give crowns and pounds and guineas
   But not your heart away;
Give pearls away and rubies
   But keep your fancy free.'
But I was one-and-twenty,
   No use to talk to me.

When I was one-and-twenty
   I heard him say again,
'The heart out of the bosom
   Was never given in vain;
'Tis paid with sighs a plenty
   And sold for endless rue.'
And I am two-and-twenty,
   And oh, 'tis true, 'tis true.

**<Text 3>** Wilfred Owen, 'Futility' (1918)

Move him into the sun —
Gently its touch awoke him once,
At home, whispering of fields unsown.
Always it woke him, even in France,
Until this morning and this snow.
If anything might rouse him now
The kind old sun will know.

Think how it wakes the seeds, —
Woke, once, the clays of a cold star.
Are limbs, so dear-achieved, are sides,
Full-nerved — still warm — too hard to stir?
Was it for this the clay grew tall?
— O what made fatuous sunbeams toil
To break earth's sleep at all?

## ●詩人の視点のありか

**<Text 1>** Alfred Tennyson, 'The Eagle' (執筆 1833)

He clasps the crag with crooked hands;
Close to the sun in lonely lands,
Ring'd with the azure world, he stands.

The wrinkled sea beneath him crawls;
He watches from his mountain walls,
And like a thunderbolt he falls.

**<Text 2>**  James Russell Lowell, 'The Fountain' (1844)

Into the sunshine,
   Full of the light,
Leaping and flashing
   From morn till night!

Into the moonlight,
   Whiter than snow,
Waving so flower-like
   When the winds blow!

Into the starlight
   Rushing in spray,
Happy at midnight,
   Happy by day!

Ever in motion,
   Blithesome and cheery
Still climbing heavenward,
   Never aweary; —

Glad of all weathers,
   Still seeming best,
Upward and downward,
   Motion thy rest; —

Full of a nature
   Nothing can tame,
Changed every moment,
   Ever the same; —

Ceaseless aspiring,
   Ceaseless content,
Darkness of sunshine
   Thy element; —

Glorious fountain!
   Let my heart be
Fresh, changeful, constant,
   Upward, like thee!

# 4. 自分のことを語る

## ●思い出をめぐる語り

**&lt;Text 1&gt;** Charles Darwin, from *The Autobiography of Charles Darwin* (1887)

I was born at Shrewsbury on February 12th, 1809, and my earliest recollection goes back only to when I was a few months over four years old, when we went to near Abergele for sea-bathing, and I recollect some events and places there with some little distinctness.

My mother died in July 1817, when I was a little over eight years old, and it is odd that I can remember hardly anything about her except her deathbed, her black velvet gown, and her curiously constructed work-table. In the spring of this same year I was sent to a day-school in Shrewsbury, where I stayed a year. I have been told that I was much slower in learning than my younger sister Catherine, and I believe that I was in many ways a naughty boy.

By the time I went to this day-school my taste for natural history, and more especially for collecting, was well developed. I tried to make out the names of plants, and collected all sorts of things, shells, seals, franks, coins, and minerals. The passion for collecting which leads a man to be a systematic naturalist, a virtuoso, or a miser, was very strong in me, and was clearly innate, as none of my sisters or brother ever had this taste.

One little event during this year has fixed itself very firmly in my mind, and I hope that it has done so from my conscience having been afterwards sorely troubled by it; it is curious as showing that apparently I was interested at this early age in the variability of plants! I told another little boy (I believe it was Leighton, who afterwards became a well-known lichenologist and botanist) that I could produce variously coloured polyanthuses and primroses by watering them with certain coloured fluids, which was of course a monstrous fable, and had never been tried by me. I may here also confess that as a little boy I was much given to inventing deliberate falsehoods, and this was always done for the sake of causing excitement. For instance, I once gathered much valuable fruit from my father's trees and hid it in the shrubbery, and then ran in breathless haste to spread the news that I had discovered a hoard of stolen fruit.

# Appendix

<Text 2> L. M. Montgomery, from the diary of August 16, 1907, *The Selected Journals of L. M. Montgomery*, Vol. 1 (1985)

All my life it has been my aim to write a book — a "real live" book. Of late years I have been thinking of it seriously but somehow it seemed such a big task I hadn't the courage to begin it. I have always hated *beginning* a story. When I get the first paragraph written I feel as though it were half done. To begin a *book* therefore seemed a quite enormous undertaking. Besides, I did not see just how I could get time for it. I could not afford to take time from my regular work to write it.

I have always kept a notebook in which I jotted down, as they occurred to me, ideas for plots, incidents, characters and descriptions. Two years ago in the spring of 1905 I was looking over this notebook in search of some suitable idea for a short serial I wanted to write for a certain Sunday School paper and I found a faded entry, written ten years before: — "Elderly couple apply to orphan asylum for a boy. By mistake a girl is sent them." I thought this would do. I began to block out chapters, devise incidents and "brood up" my heroine. Somehow or other she seemed very real to me and took possession of me to an unusual extent. Her personality appealed to me and I thought it rather a shame to waste her on an ephemeral little serial. Then the thought came, "Write a book about her. You have the central idea and character. All you have to do is to spread it out over enough chapters to amount to a book."

The result of this was "Anne of Green Gables".

I began the actual writing of it one evening in May and wrote most of it in the evenings after my regular work was done, through that summer and autumn, finishing it, I think, sometime in January 1906. It was a labor of love. Nothing I have ever written gave me so much pleasure to write. I cast "moral" and "Sunday School" ideals to the winds and made my "Anne" a real human girl. Many of my own childhood experiences and dreams were worked up into its chapters. Cavendish scenery supplied the background and *Lover's Lane* figures very prominently. There is plenty of incident in it but after all it must stand or fall by "Anne". *She* is the book.

## ●小説の登場人物の語り

**<Text 1>**   Charles Dickens, from Chapter 1, *David Copperfield* (1849–50)

I was born at Blunderstone, in Suffolk, or 'thereby,' as they say in Scotland. I was a posthumous child. My father's eyes had closed upon the light of this world six months, when mine opened on it. There is something strange to me, even now, in the reflection that he never saw me; and something stranger yet in the shadowy remembrance that I have of my first childish associations with his white grave-stone in the churchyard, and of the indefinable compassion I used to feel for it lying out alone there in the dark night, when our little parlour was warm and bright with fire and candle, and the doors of our house were — almost cruelly, it seemed to me sometimes — bolted and locked against it.

**<Text 2>**   Charlotte Brontë, from Chapter 21, *Jane Eyre* (1847)

When I was a little girl, only six years old, I, one night, heard Bessie Leaven say to Martha Abbot that she had been dreaming about a little child; and that to dream of children was a sure sign of trouble, either to one's self or one's kin. The saying might have worn out of my memory, had not a circumstance immediately followed which served indelibly to fix it there. The next day Bessie was sent for home to the deathbed of her little sister.

Of late I had often recalled this saying and this incident; for during the past week scarcely a night had gone over my couch that had not brought with it a dream of an infant: which I sometimes hushed in my arms, sometimes dandled on my knee, sometimes watched playing with daisies on a lawn; or again, dabbling its hands in running water. It was a wailing child this night, and a laughing one the next: now it nestled close to me, and now it ran from me; but whatever mood the apparition evinced, whatever aspect it wore, it failed not for seven successive nights to meet me the moment I entered the land of slumber.

**<Text 3>**   Mary Shelley, from Volume 2, Chapter 3, *Frankenstein* (1818)

'It was dark when I awoke; I felt cold also, and half-frightened as it were instinctively, finding myself so desolate. Before I had quitted your apartment, on a sensation of cold, I had covered myself with some clothes; but these were insufficient to secure me from the dews of night. I was a poor, helpless, miserable wretch; I knew, and could distinguish, nothing; but, feeling pain invade me on all sides, I sat down and wept.

'Soon a gentle light stole over the heavens, and gave me a sensation of pleasure. I started up, and beheld a radiant form rise from among the trees. I gazed with a kind of wonder. It moved slowly, but it enlightened my path; and I again went out in search of berries. I was still cold, when under one of the trees I found a huge cloak, with which I covered myself, and sat down upon the ground. No distinct ideas occupied my mind; all was confused. I felt light, and hunger, and thirst, and darkness; innumerable sounds rung in my ears, and on all sides various scents saluted me: the only object that I could distinguish was the bright moon, and I fixed my eyes on that with pleasure.

'Several changes of day and night passed, and the orb of night had greatly lessened when I began to distinguish my sensations from each other. I gradually saw plainly the clear stream that supplied me with drink, and the trees that shaded me with their foliage. I was delighted when I first discovered that a pleasant sound, which often saluted my ears, proceeded from the throats of the little winged animals who had often intercepted the light from my eyes. I began also to observe, with greater accuracy, the forms that surrounded me, and to perceive the boundaries of the radiant roof of light which canopied me. Sometimes I tried to imitate the pleasant songs of the birds, but was unable. Sometimes I wished to express my sensations in my own mode, but the uncouth and inarticulate sounds which broke from me frightened me into silence again.

'The moon had disappeared from the night, and again, with a lessened form, shewed itself, while I still remained in the forest. My sensations had, by this time, become distinct, and my mind received every day additional ideas. My eyes became accustomed to the light, and to perceive objects in their right forms; I distinguished the insect from the herb, and, by degrees, one herb from another. I found that the sparrow uttered none but harsh notes, whilst those of the blackbird and thrush were sweet and enticing.

# 5. 人生への洞察を読む

Ralph Waldo Emerson, from "Self-Reliance" (1841)

Man is timid and apologetic; he is no longer upright; he dares not say "I think," "I am," but quotes some saint or sage. He is ashamed before the blade of grass or the blowing rose. These roses under my window make no reference to former roses or to better ones; they are for what they are; they exist with God to-day. There is no time to them. There is simply the rose; it is perfect in every moment of its existence. Before a leaf-bud has burst, its whole life acts; in the full-blown flower there is no more; in the leafless root there is no less. Its nature is satisfied, and it satisfies nature, in all moments alike. But man postpones or remembers; he does not live in the present, but with reverted eye laments the past, or, heedless of the riches that surround him, stands on tiptoe to foresee the future. He cannot be happy and strong until he too lives with nature in the present, above time.

# 6. 1篇の民話を英語で読む

Lafcadio Hearn, 'Yuki-Onna' in *Kwaidan: Stories and Studies of Strange Things* (1904)

In a village of Musashi Province, there lived two woodcutters: Mosaku and Minokichi. At the time of which I am speaking, Mosaku was an old man; and Minokichi, his apprentice, was a lad of eighteen years. Every day they went together to a forest situated about five miles from their village. On the way to that forest there is a wide river to cross; and there is a ferry-boat. Several times a bridge was built where the ferry is; but the bridge was each time carried away by a flood. No common bridge can resist the current there when the river rises.

Mosaku and Minokichi were on their way home, one very cold evening, when a great snowstorm overtook them. They reached the ferry; and they found that the boatman had gone away, leaving his boat on the other side of the river. It was no day for swimming; and the woodcutters took shelter in the ferryman's hut, — thinking themselves lucky to find any shelter at all. There was no brazier in the hut, nor any place in which to make a fire: it was only a two-mat[†] hut, with a single door, but no window. Mosaku and Minokichi fastened the door, and lay down to rest, with their straw rain-coats over them. At first they did not feel very cold; and they thought that the storm would soon be over.

The old man almost immediately fell asleep; but the boy, Minokichi, lay awake a long time, listening to the awful wind, and the continual slashing of the snow against the door. The river was roaring; and the hut swayed and creaked like a junk at sea. It was a terrible storm; and the air was every moment becoming colder; and Minokichi shivered under his rain-coat. But at last, in spite of the cold, he too fell asleep.

He was awakened by a showering of snow in his face. The door of the hut had been forced open; and, by the snow-light (*yuki-akari*), he saw a woman in the room, — a woman all in white. She was bending above Mosaku, and blowing her breath upon

---

[†] That is to say, with a floor-surface of about six feet square.

him; — and her breath was like a bright white smoke. Almost in the same moment she turned to Minokichi, and stooped over him. He tried to cry out, but found that he could not utter any sound. The white woman bent down over him, lower and lower, until her face almost touched him; and he saw that she was very beautiful, — though her eyes made him afraid. For a little time she continued to look at him; — then she smiled, and she whispered: — "I intended to treat you like the other man. But I cannot help feeling some pity for you, — because you are so young. . . . You are a pretty boy, Minokichi; and I will not hurt you now. But, if you ever tell anybody — even your own mother — about what you have seen this night, I shall know it; and then I will kill you. . . . Remember what I say!"

With these words, she turned from him, and passed through the doorway. Then he found himself able to move; and he sprang up, and looked out. But the woman was nowhere to be seen; and the snow was driving furiously into the hut. Minokichi closed the door, and secured it by fixing several billets of wood against it. He wondered if the wind had blown it open; — he thought that he might have been only dreaming, and might have mistaken the gleam of the snow-light in the doorway for the figure of a white woman: but he could not be sure. He called to Mosaku, and was frightened because the old man did not answer. He put out his hand in the dark, and touched Mosaku's face, and found that it was ice! Mosaku was stark and dead. . . .

By dawn the storm was over; and when the ferryman returned to his station, a little after sunrise, he found Minokichi lying senseless beside the frozen body of Mosaku. Minokichi was promptly cared for, and soon came to himself; but he remained a long time ill from the effects of the cold of that terrible night. He had been greatly frightened also by the old man's death; but he said nothing about the vision of the woman in white. As soon as he got well again, he returned to his calling, — going alone every morning to the forest, and coming back at nightfall with his bundles of wood, which his mother helped him to sell.

One evening, in the winter of the following year, as he was on his way home, he overtook a girl who happened to be traveling by the same road. She was a tall, slim girl, very good-looking; and she answered Minokichi's greeting in a voice as pleasant to the ear as the voice of a song-bird. Then he walked beside her; and they began to talk. The girl said that her name was O-Yuki;‡ that she had lately lost both of her parents; and that she was going to Yedo, where she happened to have some poor relations, who might help her to find a situation as servant. Minokichi soon felt charmed by this strange girl; and the more that he looked at her, the handsomer she appeared to be. He asked her whether she was yet betrothed; and she answered, laughingly, that she was free. Then, in her turn, she asked Minokichi whether he was married, or pledged to marry; and he told her that, although he had only a widowed mother to support, the question of an "honorable daughter-in-law" had not yet been considered, as he was very young. . . . After these confidences, they walked on for a long while without speaking; but, as the proverb declares, *Ki ga aréba, mé mo kuchi hodo ni mono wo iu*: "When the wish is there, the eyes can say as much as the mouth." By the time they reached the village, they had become very much pleased with each other; and then Minokichi asked O-Yuki to rest awhile at his house. After some shy hesitation, she went there with him; and his mother made her welcome, and prepared a warm meal for her. O-Yuki behaved so nicely that Minokichi's mother took a sudden fancy to her, and persuaded her to delay her journey to Yedo. And the natural end of the matter was that Yuki never went to Yedo at all. She remained in the house, as an "honorable daughter-in-law."

O-Yuki proved a very good daughter-in-law. When Minokichi's mother came to die, — some five years later, — her last words were words of affection and praise for the wife of her son. And O-Yuki bore Minokichi ten children, boys and girls, — handsome children all of them, and very fair of skin.

The country-folk thought O-Yuki a wonderful person, by nature different from themselves. Most of the peasant-women age early; but O-Yuki, even after having become the mother of ten children, looked as young and fresh as on the day when she had first come to the village.

---

‡ This name, signifying "Snow," is not uncommon. On the subject of Japanese female names, see my paper in the volume entitled *Shadowings*.

One night, after the children had gone to sleep, O-Yuki was sewing by the light of a paper lamp; and Minokichi, watching her, said: —

"To see you sewing there, with the light on your face, makes me think of a strange thing that happened when I was a lad of eighteen. I then saw somebody as beautiful and white as you are now — indeed, she was very like you." . . .

Without lifting her eyes from her work, O-Yuki responded: —

"Tell me about her. . . . Where did you see her?"

Then Minokichi told her about the terrible night in the ferryman's hut, — and about the White Woman that had stooped above him, smiling and whispering, — and about the silent death of old Mosaku. And he said: —

"Asleep or awake, that was the only time that I saw a being as beautiful as you. Of course, she was not a human being; and I was afraid of her, — very much afraid, — but she was so white! . . . Indeed, I have never been sure whether it was a dream that I saw, or the Woman of the Snow." . . .

O-Yuki flung down her sewing, and arose, and bowed above Minokichi where he sat, and shrieked into his face: —

"It was I — I — I! Yuki it was! And I told you then that I would kill you if you ever said one word about it! . . . But for those children asleep there, I would kill you this moment! And now you had better take very, very good care of them; for if ever they have reason to complain of you, I will treat you as you deserve!" . . .

Even as she screamed, her voice became thin, like a crying of wind; — then she melted into a bright white mist that spired to the roof-beams, and shuddered away through the smoke-hole. . . . Never again was she seen.

# Acknowledgements

Session 2 — *The Penguin Dictionary of Jokes, Wisecracks, Quips and Quotes*, compiled by Fred Metcalf (Viking, 1993). Copyright © Fred Metcalf, 1993. Reproduced by permission of Penguin Books Ltd.

Session 3 — The Society of Authors, on behalf of the Bernard Shaw Estate.

Session 4 — 宮沢賢治著、ジョン・ベスター訳『ベスト・オブ宮沢賢治短編集』（講談社インターナショナル、1996）; *Rashomon and Seventeen Other Stories by Ryunosuke Akutagawa*, translated by Jay Rubin with an introduction by Haruki Murakami (Penguin Books, 2006). Translation copyright © Jay Rubin, 2006. Reproduced by permission of Penguin Books Ltd.

Session 5 — LUKA By SUZANNE VEGA © 1987 WB MUSIC CORP. and WAIFERSONGS LTD. All rights administered by WB MUSIC CORP. All Rights Reserved Used by Permission.

Session 6 — Martin Luther King, Jr., edited by Clayborne Carson, *The Autobiography of Martin Luther King, Jr.* (Warner Books, 1998).

Session 7 — Graham Greene, *A Sort of Life* (Vintage, 1999).

Session 8 — Raymond Carver, *Where I'm Calling From: new and selected stories* (Vintage, 1989).

Session 9 — William J. Higginson, *The Haiku Handbook: How to Write, Share, and Teach Haiku* (Kodansha International, 1985); Basho Matsuo, translated by Donald Keene, *The Narrow Road to Oku* (Kodansha International, 1996); アーサー・ビナード著『日本語ぽこりぽこり』（小学館、2005）; 谷川俊太郎『コカコーラ・レッスン』（思潮社、1980）; Shuntaro Tanikawa, *Selected Poems*, translated by William I. Elliott and Kazuo Kawamura (Persea Books, 2001); アーサー・ビナード著『日本の名詩、英語でおどる』（みすず書房、2007）.

Session 10 — Brendan Kennelly, *Reservoir Voices* (Bloodaxe Books, 2009); Robert Pinsky, *Jersey Rain* (Farrar Straus Giroux, 2000); Copyright Siegfried Sassoon by kind permission of the Estate of George Sassoon.

Session 11 — *Tennessee Williams: Plays 1937–1955*, ed. Mel Gussow and Kenneth Holdich, Library of America Series, Vol. 1 (New Directions Publishing, 2000).

Session 13 — Tim O'Brien, *The Things They Carried* (Flamingo, 1991).

Session 14 — Copyright © 2002 by Paul Auster, published by Picador. Reprinted with permission of the Carol Mann Agency.

〈編注者紹介〉

斎藤兆史（さいとう・よしふみ）
　東京大学名誉教授。東京大学文学部英語・英米文学科卒業、同大学院人文科学研究科英文学専門課程修士課程修了、インディアナ大学英文科修士課程修了、ノッティンガム大学英文科博士課程修了 (Ph.D)。主な著書に、『英語達人列伝』、『英語達人塾』（ともに中央公論新社）、『日本人と英語』（研究社）、訳書に『少年キム』（ラドヤード・キプリング著、晶文社）、『ある放浪者の半生』、『魔法の種』（ともに V・S・ナイポール著、岩波書店）ほか。

中村哲子（なかむら・てつこ）
　駒澤大学総合教育研究部教授。ノッティンガム大学英文科修士課程修了、慶應義塾大学大学院博士課程修了後、日本医科大学勤務を経て現職。主な著書（共著）に、『身体医文化論』（慶應義塾大学出版会）、『チョーサーと英米文学』（金星堂）、『英語の教え方学び方』（東京大学出版会）、*Literature and Language Learning in the EFL Classroom* (Palgrave Macmillan)、*Big Dipper Writing Course* （高等学校検定教科書、数研出版）ほか。

KENKYUSHA
〈検印省略〉

## English through Literature
（文学で学ぶ英語リーディング）

2009 年 11 月 1 日　初版発行　　2023 年 11 月 30 日　　9 刷発行

| 編注者 | 斎　藤　兆　史 |
|---|---|
|  | 中　村　哲　子 |
| 発行者 | 吉　田　尚　志 |
| 発行所 | 株式会社 研 究 社 |

〒102-8152　東京都千代田区富士見 2-11-3
電話　03-3288-7711（編集）
　　　03-3288-7777（営業）
振替　00150-9-26710
研究社ホームページ　https://www.kenkyusha.co.jp/

印刷所　図書印刷株式会社

装丁　清水良洋　　本文デザイン　Informe（インフォルム）

©2009, Saito Yoshifumi and Nakamura Tetsuko　　Printed in Japan
ISBN978-4-327-42185-4 C1082